SURVIVAL!
IN THE MOUNTAINS

SURVIVAL!
IN THE MOUNTAINS

KEN McMURTRY

Illustrated by Rose Water

AN AVON CAMELOT BOOK

For John and Jan McMurtry

SURVIVAL! IN THE MOUNTAINS is an original publication of Avon Books. This work has never before appeared in book form.

AVON BOOKS
A division of
The Hearst Corporation
1350 Avenue of the Americas
New York, New York 10019

Library of Congress Cataloging in Publication Data:

McMurtry, Ken.
   Survival! in the mountains / Ken McMurtry.
      p.   cm.
Includes bibliographical references.
Summary: Presents facts about mountains and information necessary for survival when mountain climbing.
1. Wilderness survival—Juvenile literature. 2. Mountaineering—Juvenile literature. [1. Mountaineering. 2. Wilderness survival. 3. Survival.] I. Title.
GV200.5.M38   1993
613.6'9—dc20   92-31930   CIP   AC

First Avon Camelot Printing: March 1993

CAMELOT TRADEMARK REG. U.S. PAT. OFF. AND IN OTHER COUNTRIES, MARCA REGISTRADA, HECHO EN U.S.A.

Printed in the U.S.A.

OPM   10 9 · 8   7   6   5   4   3   2   1

Contents

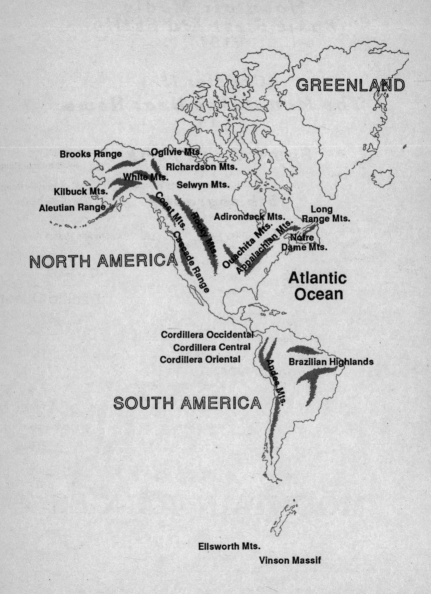

MOUNTAIN RANGES

Chapter 1

The Mountain

It started to snow in the late afternoon. It wasn't supposed to. This was southern California, after all. And the weatherman had said it would be warm and sunny. But that was eight hours earlier and almost ten thousand feet lower down the mountain. The three boys hadn't paid much attention then. They had been on hikes before, so an overnight camping trip didn't seem like that big a deal to the two older boys.

Charlie and Paul had been good friends for ten of their seventeen years. They had done a lot of things together. This, however, was the first time either one of them had been mountain camping. The youngest boy, Charlie's kid brother Ken, was only eleven. To him the trip *was* a big deal, but he didn't worry about things like the weather. He knew that Charlie would take care of him. He always had.

Ken had bragged about his mountain-climbing adventure to his classmates for days before the trip. For a shy sixth-grader who had never been more than a few feet above sea level in his life, this first night away seemed like a dream come true. Mt. San Gorgonio had taken on mythical proportions for him. He was going to be the conquering hero.

The first few hours of the hike had met Ken's expectations. He felt grand in his brand-new boots and his loaded pack. This outdoors stuff was all right. That is, it was all right until lunchtime. It was then that his feet began hurting him.

By midafternoon, blisters had appeared on his heels. He didn't want to complain; he had nagged Charlie into bringing him, and now he didn't want to seem a burden. Next time, he would break in his boots before hiking all day.

By midafternoon, too, his legs had become shaky under the weight of his pack. He had to be careful not to lose his balance. The trail was only a few inches wide in places, on the edge of cliff-like drop-offs.

Late in the day, when the first drops of cold moisture started forming in the air, Ken felt scared. It was then he realized Charlie and Paul were nervous about their situation; they didn't have all the answers. They had never been camping in the snow. In fact, they didn't know any more than he did what to do when caught in a blizzard ten thousand feet up in the air.

They argued about whether to turn back, keep going, or set up camp. And then, right in the middle of their heated discussion, they both looked into Ken's fear-widened eyes and suddenly burst into uncontrollable laughter. Was their giddiness the first sign of altitude sickness? The lack of oxygen at higher altitudes, where the air is thinner, can cause light-headedness, headaches, and sometimes even nausea. Climbers of high mountains often have to stop during an ascent to adjust to the altitude.

Of course, an overnight trip up and down southern California's second highest (at 11,502 feet) mountain didn't leave the three boys much time to adjust to changes in the altitude.

They finally decided to make camp while they were still below the timberline. It was getting too dark to do anything else. The droplets turned into real snow while they were setting up the tents. Paul had brought along a one-man tent shaped like a coffin. Charlie had brought a two-man pup tent to share with Ken. They had been hot all day from hiking. Now it was turning very cold. When the tents were set up, the three huddled in the pup tent peeking out of the flaps. The snow fell in huge wet flakes, fast and thick.

They couldn't build a camp fire. It was illegal to build open fires on Mt. San Gorgonio. Even if it weren't, the snow had covered everything. They did have a can of Sterno—a kind of jellied alcohol which burns slowly. In the opening of the tent, Charlie cooked dinner, a pot of dehydrated vegetable soup mixed with snow and heated over the canned heat to almost warm. The vegetables were very chewy, but the boys were too tired to care. Tired and cold.

They ate chocolate bars and watched from the safety of the tent as the white blizzard swirled around them. The snow was piling up on the ground. In the few hours since sunset, several inches had fallen. The branches of evergreen trees surrounding the clearing where they had pitched their tents hung bent toward the earth, heavy with snow.

The boys sat in the dark. The silence of the snow was everywhere. It was bedtime. Paul slipped out of the pup tent into the white wall of swirling snow to climb into his sleeping bag in his own small tent.

Ken took his boots off, slowly peeling away the cold,

sweat-soaked socks from his feet. Three large red blisters on the heel of his right foot and two on the heel of his left made tight little mounds of sensitive skin. His teeth chattered from the cold. His brother advised him to put on more layers of clothing to keep warm, but his knapsack held more books than clothes. Next time, he would pay more attention to his packing. Charlie put the lid on the can of Sterno, and they were in total darkness. Charlie then tied the tent flaps shut to keep the snow out and their body heat in. Ken missed his night-light and electric blanket. Somehow, the darkness, so dense and total, was even more frightening than the cold and snow.

In the morning, they discovered three disturbing things. The first was that the snow had stopped, but at least ten inches had fallen in the night. Walking down the mountain would be like wading through honey, and dangerously slippery besides. The second was that all their food was missing. Paul had left the food pack outside the door of his tent, covered by a small piece of canvas. The third was Ken's boots. Ken tried putting them on, but couldn't. They were frozen. Much to Charlie's and Paul's disgust, he had neglected to put them in his sleeping bag with him overnight. He had left them by the tent flap.

Charlie put a match to the Sterno and managed to thaw the boots somewhat by holding them over the thin, blue flame. When they were flexible enough to pull on, Ken tugged them gingerly onto his tender feet. His blisters burned with pain as the stiff cold leather rubbed against them. Cold, wearing half-frozen boots, the snow as deep as his knees, Ken wondered how he would ever make it down the mountain.

A noise in the woods, down the trail from their camp,

startled the three boys. Paul was the first to suggest an animal, a bear or a mountain lion.

It was a rescue team. Two rangers appeared on the path; they were wearing small snowshoes. They carried what looked like a long aluminum pole wrapped in cloth. Charlie and Paul were thinking that there was only one thing worse than being lost in the mountains, and that was having to be rescued because of stupid mistakes. One of the few things they had done right was to register at the rangers' station before they began their climb.

But for Ken, his embarrassment was overshadowed by immense relief and the realization that he would indeed survive. He even got to ride down the mountain. The rangers realized how painfully slow the walk down the mountain would be for him. The first ranger dropped the cloth-and-aluminum contraption on the snow. With the help of his partner, he unfurled a small stretcher. Ken climbed on.

The trip down the mountain was much faster than the climb up. The snow-covered ground soon gave way to a pine-bordered path after they had descended a few hundred feet. The spring air was warm, and near the base of the mountain the mosquitoes were biting. It was good to feel safe again, aching feet and all. Ken felt like he was one hundred years old.

If you haven't guessed already, this story is about my first camping trip in the mountains. Later, I did make it to the top of Mt. San Gorgonio. By then, I knew how to be safe in the mountains. In a way, I should thank my brother for being such a terrible mountain man. That trip convinced me that I should never go into the mountains without the ability to survive under any circumstances. It was the beginning of a wonderful education.

I sometimes wished that I knew a wise, old—or young—Native American who could teach me everything about the magic and mystery of mountain nature. But I never met this person. I learned about the mountains and survival from books and practice. You can, too. You will learn a lot about what you need to know to be safe in the mountains. Plus, you will learn some neat facts about how mountains came into existence and their importance in the earth's ecological system. Finally, as you read, you will see just how many mistakes we did make in climbing Mt. San Gorgonio.

Chapter 2

Mountain Making

To learn how to be safe in the mountains you need to know about mountains themselves. Mountains may be more fascinating than you think. There are many questions about mountains, and some of the answers may surprise you.

What is a mountain?

One simple dictionary definition (*Webster's Ninth New Collegiate*) says a mountain is "a landmass that projects conspicuously above its surroundings and is higher than a hill." But beyond that, mountains can be very different. Some mountains are old and some are young. They come in all shapes and sizes. Some mountains look sharp and craggy. Some line up like the teeth on a saw. Some are horn-shaped and others are domed. Some older mountains, like the Green Mountains of Vermont and the Blue Ridge Mountains of Virginia and North Carolina, are low and rounded.

Mountains exist in a variety of climates. There are dry, desert mountains. There are wet, green, tropical mountains. And there are high, snowy mountains. Even so, there is one thing that is common to all mountains: they are warmer at the base than at the top.

The Appalachians in North Carolina are an example of folded moutains.

Why is it colder at the top. Aren't you nearer the sun?

This is a good question. It is true that as you move higher up the mountain the temperature becomes lower. This is because the air is drier the higher you go. Drier air holds less of the warming, infrared rays of the sun. Some scientists have even calculated that the temperature drops about three degrees Fahrenheit for every thousand feet of altitude. If you're at a high altitude for any length of time, it is a good idea to wear sun block and good sunglasses. Even though it is cooler, the sun's ultraviolet rays are much stronger. These are the rays that cause sunburn, so you burn more easily.

Imagine a mountain as a many-layered cake, each layer a thousand feet thick. As you move from layer to layer, either up or down, the change in temperature and quality of sunlight results in tiny changes in the plants and animals that live on that layer of the mountain.

Because of this rapid climate change, mountains are places where scientists can study a thing called adaptability. They're trying to figure out why some plants and animals can adapt to changes in temperature and altitude better than others.

Have there always been mountains?

Probably not. There are several theories about the creation of the earth and the birth of mountains. Whichever theory you choose to believe (more on a couple of theories later in this chapter), there is agreement that the first granite peak probably appeared at least three billion years ago.

People who try to determine the ages of mountains are like detectives; they study clues and make guesses based on scientific knowledge.

The clues they study are the fossil remains of plants and animals that are found in the sedimentary rocks of nonvolcanic peaks. Scientists know that different plants and animals lived at different times during the development of the earth. Here's the tricky part. Many of the fossils found on the tops of mountains have been aquatic—sea life. This means the living thing existed at sea level before being lifted to the top of the mountain. What is now a mountaintop once existed on the ocean or lake floor.

This study of fossils has been mapped according to historical evidence and is called the fossil record. Using this method, a vast calendar of the past, before man lived on earth, has been constructed by geologists and paleobotanists. You may have seen one of these fossil record charts in your classroom at school, or at a museum.

Who came up with the idea of the fossil record?

It was only about two hundred years ago that the idea occurred to a titled Frenchman named Comte de Buffon. He became fascinated by the seashells he found embedded in the rocks and hillsides of France. After a great deal of thought, he suggested that sea animals had once lived at the places where these mountains now stood.

His famous friend, the writer-philosopher Voltaire, was skeptical. He thought the notion of a mountain rising up from the earth preposterous. Voltaire's explanation was that over the years tourists from the seaside had carried the shells up the mountains on outings and had left them there.

Voltaire later agreed with Buffon's theory that soft sediments had covered these sea creatures and hardened into rocks that were later lifted high above sea level.

Later, scientifically-advanced fossil records divided the three ages of animals into the Paleozoic, Mesozoic, and Cenozoic periods. The Paleozoic era began about 620 million years ago. This was the first record of marine creatures being preserved. First came jellyfish,

Another example of folded mountains in the Mt. Mitchell Game Area of North Carolina. Notice how the mountains form a folded pattern, as if they were part of a piece of stiff material.

(Courtesy North Carolina Wildlife Resources Commission, Jack Dermid)

soft-bodied worms, and other invertebrate sea animals, and later fishes, insects, reptiles, and amphibians. The Mesozoic era, the time of "intermediate animals," is probably best known as the time of the dinosaurs, but it also saw the earliest birds and mammals. It began about 230 million years ago and lasted until the Cenozoic era, 70 million years ago. The Cenozoic period is when the "recent animals" first appeared on earth. Fos-

11

sils of men and women and children show that humans lived only within the last two million years.

Scientists believe that at least three different periods of mountain-building occurred before the Paleozoic era, and several others since.

They're guessing. But the guess is based on two things. First, evidence of at least three different mountainous areas has been discovered where there are *no* fossil remains. The notion is that these mountains emerged before fossils existed. The second reason to believe that the three mountain chains came into existence at different periods is erosion. The mountains are at different stages in their aging process.

What is this aging process?

The mountains that you see today will not appear to change in your lifetime. Geologists think of mountains as having a life cycle like humans. The cycle of a mountain is birth, youth, long maturity, long old age, and finally death when it is worn down. From the moment a mountain comes into existence it begins aging. The geologists and other scientists who study the life of mountains talk of them as being "young" or "old." The truth is that mountains do age, but the process is almost impossible to imagine. A day for us would probably be the equivalent of a million years for a mountain.

What age a mountain are erosion and the leveling force of gravity. Erosion is the wearing down of the mountain's surface by wind and water. Gravity is the invisible force which holds us to the earth. The taller mountains ranges, like the Himalayas, are the young mountains. Ranges that have been worn down to a rolling roundness, like the Pocono Mountains in Pennsylvania, are the older mountains.

Is erosion bad?

No. When the continents were first formed on this planet, the surface was probably a light granite rock. As mountains thrust up from the earth, they offered the possibility of erosion. Why? The mountainside became a place for the wind to work, breaking off small pieces of stone which would eventually slide to the base of the mountain. Because mountains have sloped sides, rainwater carried these bits of granite down the mountain. Because of the steep slopes, rainwater also created streambeds and canyons. The water and wind worked together to break the granite rock into smaller and smaller pieces. As it was washed down the mountain, it was ground and crumbled into sand and dust. These first mountains then provided the raw materials for our soil.

After a period of soil creation, sea plants could take root on the newly-created soil—topsoil—on the continents. Remember, this took millions of years.

Erosion and gravity also create an environment that encourages future mountain building. Geologists now understand that the slow process whereby weight is shifted from the mountains toward the ocean floor creates disturbances in the balance of the earth's crust starting the process over again.

Well, how do mountains begin?

Different types of mountains are formed by different processes. For example, you probably could guess that volcanic action is one way mountains are formed. Mt.

St. Helens's eruption in 1980 is a scary reminder of the power of volcanic action.

To really understand the formation of mountains, we should talk a little bit about the theories of how the earth came into being. It's true that all mountains, volcanic and otherwise, have been formed because of deep forces working within the earth.

If you could slice the earth in half, like a peach, you would discover that it is layered around a solid core. The outermost layer, which we walk on, is the crust of the earth and, like the skin of the peach, is very thin

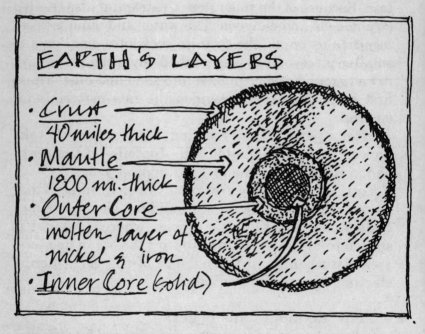

EARTH'S LAYERS

• Crust —
  40 miles thick
• Mantle —
  1800 mi. thick
• Outer Core —
  molten layer of
  nickel & iron
• Inner Core (solid)

A diagram showing the earth's layers. Disruptions between the layers, such as a volcano or earthquake, can create new mountains.

compared to the inner layers. The earth's crust varies in thickness. At its thickest, it is about forty miles deep.

Under the crust is a deeper layer called the mantle. The mantle is more than eighteen hundred miles thick, and while solid, scientists believe pliable. Just beneath the mantle is a molten layer of nickel and iron, called the outer core. The outer core is a very dense hot liquid metal. Some scientists now believe that at the very center of the earth, like the pit of the peach, is a solid inner core.

This description of the makeup of the earth's interior is mostly speculation. But scientists do know, from drilling the earth's crust and measuring temperatures, and from studying deep mines and caves, that the deeper down you measure the temperature of the earth, the hotter it gets. Geysers and volcanoes are also indications of the heat that lies beneath the world we know.

So what are the different ways mountains form?

One theory about the heat in the core of the earth is that the earth was originally a piece of the sun. This piece was spun off into orbit and began cooling down. Some scientists believe the earth is still cooling. A piece of fruit, the apple, is often used by these scientists to describe how mountains are formed. Have you ever dried a whole apple? If so, you would notice that as it dries it develops lumps and ridges and begins to look like a kind of miniature version of a relief globe.

If the earth is cooling, then a great deal of surface stress is created. This stress would produce release of pressure in some areas—volcanoes and domed mountains, which are created by volcanic action, as well as

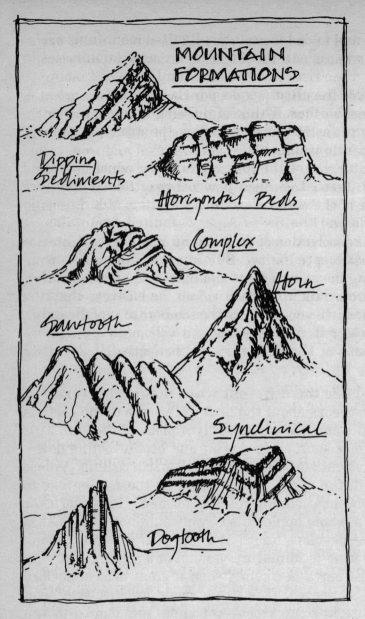

Examples of various types of mountains.

faulting and folded mountains. Faulted mountains are created when clean breaks occur in solid landmasses and one mass rises and the other sinks. Folded mountains are a result of stress which pushes two areas toward each other. Think of pushing a rug together. The humps formed are created on the same principle as folded mountains.

These, then, are the four methods by which mountains are created: 1) pushed together or folded mountains, such as the Appalachians, the Atlas Mountains, the Urals and the Swiss Alps; 2) faulted mountains, where a solid landmass is forced up along a fault line, such as the Sierra Nevada of California and the Tetons; 3) mountains created by volcanic action, where material is pushed up from deep within the earth to create a mountain through the accumulation of cinder and lava, such as Kilimanjaro in Africa, Popocatépetl and Ixtacihuatl in Mexico, Fujiyama in Japan, Vesuvius and Etna in Italy, and Mt. St. Helens in Washington state; 4) dome mountains, resulting from hot, volcanic materials trying, but failing, to reach the earth's surface. The pressure from beneath pushes up the earth, like a blister on the skin, to form a dome-shaped mountain. An example of domed mountains would be the Henry Mountains in southern Utah.

The other theory about how the earth was created agrees that mountains are created in these ways. But the theory believes the earth is heating up, not cooling down. Scientists subscribing to this other theory do not think the earth was once part of the sun. They believe that the earth is a result of enormous amounts of particles and gasses forming together in a great ball held together by gravity and motion.

The very hot temperatures at the center of the earth are attributed to pressure and radioactive materials in the rocks. This idea of millions and millions of particles coming together to form the earth may sound strange, but think about this: every year the earth is bombarded with 730,000 *tons* of meteorite particles.

How hot is the center of the earth?

No one knows. There is a guess that at over 3,000 miles deep, where the mantle meets the inner core, the temperature is around 3,000–4,000 degrees Fahrenheit.

This estimate is made based on the pressure per square inch calculated for that depth. If you have ever dived to the bottom of a swimming pool, you will understand that the pressure on your skin increases as you go deeper. If you were to go five miles down in the sea, the pressure per square inch of skin would be around 12,000 pounds. This is one reason exploring the sea is so difficult. At 1,800 miles, the pressure is calculated to be 16,950,000 pounds per square inch. This is enough pressure to turn rocks and metals into liquid and this change causes heat during the process.

Are there dates when some of these mountain ranges came into being?

Yes. Here is a list with approximate dates. It is a good idea to have a good atlas or relief globe so you can look up the ranges listed.

400 Million Years Ago: Caledonians
Highlands of Scotland
Glacier-covered mass of
    Greenland

230 Million Years Ago:	Adirondacks
	Green Mountains
	Catskills
	Great Smokies
70 Million Years Ago:	Andes
	Rocky Mountains
	Himalayas
15 Million Years Ago:	Cascade Range
	Alps in Europe
	Himalayas pushed
	higher

What about glaciers?

Glaciers are remnants of the Ice Age. In Switzerland there are many mountain valleys shaped by the movement of glaciers. These valleys are fertile and U-shaped, with steep walls rising to high peaks. Many glaciers still exist in Switzerland, high in the mountain valleys. They are fed by the snow at high altitudes, and move very slowly as the snow is incorporated into the glacier through the process of compression. Glaciers are shapers of mountains.

Mountains create topsoil by the process of erosion, and they are beautiful to look at, but is there anything else they do?

There are many things. Climate is probably the most important. By intercepting or blocking prevailing winds, mountains cause precipitation. Regions on the windward side of a great mountain range have plentiful rainfall. Those areas on the opposite side are usually arid. The shape of the invisible forces of the wind are shaped worldwide by the great mountain ranges.

An erratic boulder, deposited in the middle of rolling fields with no other mountains or rocks in sight by an ancient glacier.

(Neg. No. 323843, Photo: Logan and Rota, Courtesy Department of Library Services, American Museum of Natural History)

If you look at a globe, you will see that often borders are determined by mountains. This goes back to ancient times when transportation was more difficult. Crossing the mountains was an effort requiring both courage and resources. Because of this, mountains offered a natural protection for various populations of the world.

As natural barriers, mountains have determined the paths of traders, migrants, and invading armies. The difficulty of passage has also preserved many local customs, costumes, and beliefs.

Anything else?

Our own Gold Rush and countless others through the centuries. Mountains frequently contain veins of valuable mineral ores.

What is the highest point on earth?

Probably Mount Everest. In 1850, it was measured by a British group and recorded as being 29,002 feet high. In 1954, an official Indian survey measured the mountain as 29,028 feet. No one is really sure if the mountain had grown or if one of the measurements was inaccurate. In 1987, new satellite measurements showed that the Himalayan peak K–2 is 29,064 feet high—but Everest is 800 feet higher. However, the revised figures have not yet been accepted by the National Geographic Society.

What percentage of the earth is mountainous?

More than twenty-five percent of the earth's land surface is more than 3,000 feet high.

Several Celebrated Mountains

North America	*Height (ft.)*	*Fun Facts*
McKinley, Alaska	20,320	Highest on continent.
Popocatepetl, Mexico	17,887	Sacred Aztec peak.
Rainier, Washington	14,410	Volcanic peak bearing twenty-six glaciers.
Pikes Peak, Colorado	14,110	First recorded ascent 1820 (U.S.); now has auto road to summit.
Pelée, Martinique	5,243	Wiped out entire city of St. Pierre.
South America:		
Aconcagua, Argentina	22,834	World's longest drop, over nine miles from summit to mountain's base on the ocean bottom, 100 miles away.
Europe:		
Mont Blanc, France	15,771	Highest in Alps.
Wetterhorn, Switzerland	12,166	Climbed by British in 1854, marks start of "golden age" of mountaineering.

Europe (cont.)	Height (ft.)	Fun Facts
Etna, Italy	11,053	Highest active volcano in Europe.
Olympus, Greece	9,550	Abode of gods of Greek mythology.
Vesuvius, Italy	4,190	Destroyed Pompeii in 79 A.D.

Africa:		
Kilimanjaro, Tanzania	19,340	Extinct volcano.

Asia:		
Everest, Nepal	29,028	Believed to be highest in the world.
K2 (Godwin-Austen) Kashmir	28,250	Second highest in the world.
Manasu I, Nepal	26,760	First ascent 1956 (Japanese). Buddhist leader considered ascent a pilgrimage.
Annapurna I, Nepal	26,504	First "eight-thousander" conquered; scaled 1950 (French).
Ararat, Turkey	16,804	Extinct volcano. Reputed resting place of Noah's Ark.

Chapter 3

Mountain Madness

Leonardo da Vinci, a mountain climber? The craze to climb mountains goes back a long way. Even before the sixteenth century—in fact, as long ago as 1492—Antoine de Ville climbed a mountain that people said was impossible to conquer. The mountain was Mont Aiguille in the French Alps near Grenoble. After three days on the 6,880 foot summit, de Ville descended and wrote the first recorded account of the adventures of a mountain climber.

This was the first recorded incident of climbing a mountain just to reach the top. It didn't start a craze. In the sixteenth century, Leonardo da Vinci reportedly climbed to the top of one of the Pennines, the Alps between Italy and Switzerland.

The first non-Native American to climb a mountain in the U.S.A. was Darby Field of Exeter, New Hampshire. In 1642, he found two Native American guides who were willing to help him reach the summit of Mt. Washington, which at 6,288 feet is the highest peak in the Presidential Range.

In 1865, a man named Edward Whymper and six other climbers in his party reached the top of the Matterhorn,

The Paricutin Volcano. Notice the even, conical shape of this mountain's top.

(Courtesy Department of Library Services, American Museum of Natural History, Neg. No. 122278, Photo: F. H. Pough)

one of the Alps between the Swiss and Italian border. The Matterhorn is 14,690 feet high and was thought to be invincible at the time Whymper made his ascent. People thought it was invincible because of the way it looked. It is very dramatic, like a spike sticking into the sky, with very steep slopes. Of the seven people (one was a boy, the son of one of the climbers) who made the 1865 ascent, only three made their way down safely.

In Whymper's day, climbers did not have the mountain climbing equipment available today. They risked their lives roped together, trusting in surefootedness, their knowledge of the mountain, their local guides' experience, their own experience, the weather, and luck.

What killed the men on Whymper's climb was their trust in one of the climbers. A young man named Douglas Hadow presented himself as an experienced climber when he joined the climbing party. Whymper's mistake was believing him. On the way down the Matterhorn, Hadow required constant help in finding footholds from one of the guides.

The six men and the boy had begun their descent of the Matterhorn, roped together for safety, when Hadow lost his footing and slid backwards into the guide who had been helping him. Both men began falling backwards, pulling the two climbers in front of them off balance. Hearing the screams, Whymper, a man named Peter Taugwalder, and Taugwalder's young son, grabbed for rocks to prevent the fall. They held on with all their strength.

Then they felt nothing. The weight on the rope was gone. The rope had broken; they watched as their four companions slid a short way, then disappeared over the edge of a precipice, falling to their deaths. Later, Whymper learned the sad truth. Hadow had been on only three other climbs, and had a reputation for ineptitude.

In the late 1800s, mountain climbing was very popular in Europe. The British were avid climbers. With this interest, new tools for climbing were developed: the lightweight ice axe, pegs, (called pitons) that could be driven into rock or ice, and to which rings could be fastened to guide or hold rope, and crampons, clawlike attachments for boots to provide traction. These are still the tools of today's mountain climbers.

Around the turn of the twentieth century, many of the

great peaks of the world had been topped by climbers. Mountains of over twenty thousand feet were climbed in the Andes. In East Africa, climbers made their way up the side of dormant volcanoes. Mount Kabru, in the Himalayas, was conquered in 1883 by a climber named W. W. Graham. At 24,002 feet, it would hold the record for tallest mountain climbed for over fifty years.

While Graham's record was finally broken in 1930, it was not until 1950 that a Frenchman named Maurice Herzog made it to over 26,000 feet with Louis Lachemal. Herzog led a group which scaled Mt. Annapurna I in central Nepal. He was so disoriented at the top that he lost his gloves while taking pictures. A storm trapped the climbers on the way down, and Herzog and Lachemal suffered from severe exposure, leading to frostbite. When they finally reached base camp and received medical attention, Herzog was delirious. In the end, both men had to undergo extensive amputations of fingers and toes.

Why was Herzog delirious at the peak?

It was because of lack of oxygen. At sea level, oxygen makes up twenty-one percent of our air. As we climb to higher altitudes, the air gets thinner and cannot hold as much oxygen. You probably have noticed that when you are hiking in the mountains, climbing slopes may seem more difficult. If you are in pretty good shape this is probably because of the altitude. There is a smaller supply available of the oxygen needed to make muscles work.

In fact, Herzog's record would probably never have been broken if portable compressed oxygen had not been developed in the late 1940s, along with the face masks and regulators to deliver the oxygen safely to the user. As I'm sure you have guessed, this method of compressing and delivering oxygen safely also led to other breakthroughs. People began underwater exploration. Airplane pilots were able to set new altitude and speed records.

In 1953, a British group climbed the highest mountain peak in the world. Armed with compressed oxygen, New Zealander Edmund Hillary and Sherpa guide Tenzing Norkay, reached the top of Mt. Everest on May 29th. Mt. Everest had been conquered. John Hunt, the leader of the climb, and Hillary were both knighted by Queen Elizabeth II.

Synthetic rope is the newest aid to mountain climbers. It is strong, lightweight, and inexpensive. The invention of synthetic rope has not resulted in record-breaking climbs. The tallest known mountains had already been conquered. But it has resulted in safer climbing. Today, mountain climbers think of their sport as an art. The height of the mountain is not as important as how the mountain is climbed.

If you are interested in learning mountain climbing skills, you should attend one of the schools or camps or clubs in your area. Check in the yellow pages of your phone book for sporting goods stores that specialize in climbing gear. They should be able to provide you with information about the nearest training. If you can't find anything in the yellow pages, go to your local library and ask the research librarian to help you find this information.

When America was young, people climbed the mountains to get to the other side. Scouts searched for routes to make crossing the mountains possible by wagon trains. Explorers searched for wealth and the joy of experience, even for mythological fountains of youth and cities of gold. Trappers and hunters went into the mountains to

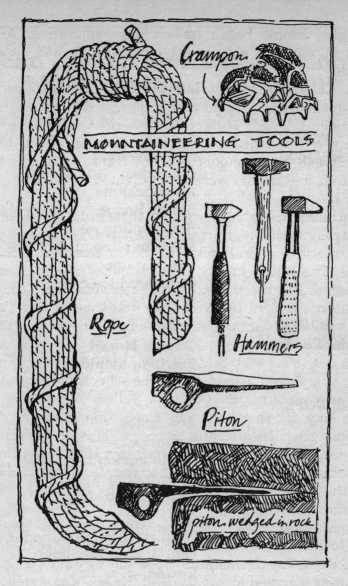

These are some of the climbing tools needed for safety in the mountains.

Principal Mountain Ranges and High Plateaus of the World

NORTH AMERICA:
Rockies
Sierra Nevada
Cascades
Appalachians
Brooks Range
Alaskan Range
Mexican plateau and
    mountains
Greenland ice cap

SOUTH AMERICA:
Andes
Gulana Massif
Brazilian highlands

EUROPE:
Alps
Apennines
Pyrenees
Scandinavian highlands
Balkan ranges
Carpathians

AFRICA:
Southern African plateaus
East African highland
Ruwenzori
Ethiopian plateau
Madagascar highlands

AFRICA:	Ahaggar
	Tibesti
	Atlas
ASIA:	Arabian plateau
	Anatolian plateau
	Caucasus
	Urals
	Plateau of Iran
	Zegros
	Elburz
	Karakoram Range
	Kunlun
	Hindu Kush
	Himalayas
	Plateau of Tibet
	Tien Shan
	Altai
	Mongolian plateau
	Kolyma
	Barisan Mountains

(Source of information, Life Nature Library, *The Mountains*)

find game. Miners went to find gold and silver and later minerals such as copper and zinc.

Today we use the mountains for recreation. People still hunt animals for their meat and fur. They fish the mountain streams for trout and bass, hoping to catch "the big one." There are still people looking for gold in the mountains. Their equipment is a bit fancier than two hundred years ago, and maybe the gold is scarcer, but the process is pleasurable. Large mining companies still look for copper and zinc as well as dozens of other minerals. And, most of us enjoy hiking, or camping, or exploring the mountains as a way of enjoying nature. Climbing the same mountain is always different.

In the winter, the mountains offer a variety of pleasures for people throughout the world who love winter sports such as skiing, sledding, or tobogganning. When snow-covered, the same slopes that aid erosion offer us speed, thrills, and a test of our skills.

To enjoy the mountains, we need to feel safe on them. That's what this book is about. Hopefully, you will never have to use the survival skills you will learn in this book, but knowing them can add to your feelings of confidence and enjoyment of the mountains.

The most important thing in any survival situation is using your head. Fear is the first reaction people experience when they find themselves in survival situations. This is normal, but easily overcome when you know what to do.

Preparation is vital. Whether you are going into the woods for a day trip or planning to spend several weeks, you should make sure people know where you are going and that you have the basics necessary for survival in an emergency.

If you find yourself in a survival situation, you must remain clearheaded. In ancient times, every day was a battle for survival, and people knew how to go about building a shelter, keeping warm, finding water and food. When you finish this book, you can practice these skills for yourself.

Here are some basic survival procedures. If you find yourself in a survival situation, you should first deter-

How Is a Mountain Measured?

In 1850, Mount Everest was measured by a team of British surveyors. The height of the mountain was determined to be 29,002 feet. In 1954, Mount Everest was measured by a team of Indian surveyors. The height of the mountain was determined to be 29,028 feet. Could it be the mountain had *grown* twenty-six feet higher between 1850 and 1954? Maybe. But then again, measuring a mountain is no easy task!

Surveyors measure mountains by first finding level spots allowing clear vertical views of the mountain. For the measurement of Everest, six of these places, called control points, were used. These control points are marked so that future surveyors can measure from the same spots. Using surveying instruments, experts measure the mountain and determine the height by averaging the measurements. These measurements can be affected by atmospheric conditions, sunlight conditions, gravitational attraction, and human error.

The newest method of measuring mountains will eventually produce accurate figures for the heights of the major mountains of the world. Cameras mounted on aircraft take overlapping pictures of mountains from above, so that they may be viewed through a 3-D viewer. Points along the mountain or range are recorded in a series. These photogrammetric recordings are then used to determine the mountain's height, contours, drainage, range area, woodland, and cultivation.

The shape, height, and contours of the mountain are determined by using complex stereoscopic plotting instruments.

mine if you or anyone else is in immediate danger. Assess the situation. If you are injured, apply first aid. Make sure equipment, food, and water are safe. Find, build, or set up shelter to protect you from the elements. Establish where water and fuel for a fire can be found. Decide whether to stay where you are or try to move to another spot.

Probably the most important rule is to live for today. Whether in a survival situation or not, you cannot dwell on what happened yesterday or worry about tomorrow. Take care of today's needs. Enjoy *today* in the mountains.

Chapter 4

A Home in the Mountains

If you were lost in the mountains, which do you think would be the most important for your survival: food, water, fire, or shelter? We can survive for several days without food, so that's not the right answer. Water is very important but, as you will see in the next chapter, there are several ways of collecting water in the mountains. Fire is the least important, unless you are in cold weather or the conditions are wet. So the first priority in a survival situation is shelter.

Fortunately, shelters are fun to build, and can be built from a variety of materials. You can practice in your own backyard or neighborhood. When building a shelter, you should be aware of location. It is best to build your shelter at the edge of a mountain clearing rather than in the woods. This is because the woods are often wet and shady. The best place for a mountain shelter is on the south side of a mountain, at the edge of a clearing where the sun's rays can warm the structure.

One question you should ask yourself before building a shelter is about size. How big should it be? The answer is that it should be adequate but small. A small shelter can more easily be built up on the outside with insulating materials, such as leaves and branches, to keep you cozy warm and dry inside. When you're out in the woods, look at shelters built by animals—squirrels' nests and birds' nests. See how they have chosen nesting sites that are protected from the elements and have built nests just large enough for their needs.

Once when I was camping in the mountains, I set up my tent on a slanting hillside and spent the evening talking with my companion. We were tired when it began to rain.

"We should have dug a trench around the tent," I said.

"The rain will blow over in a few minutes," he said.

We awoke about the same time, around 3:00 A.M., sopping wet. The rain had soaked the ground and the water had been sucked up by our sleeping bags and clothing. It was one of the most miserable nights of camping that I can remember.

This story illustrates the point that you should choose your location carefully and build the best shelter possible for your situation. It's not always possible to build a perfect shelter in a few hours before darkness. But you can always add to the shelter and make it better. In survival situations, you may not even have time to build a structure before sunset. In that situation, look for any kind of natural shelter: a cave, or rock overhang that will protect you from the elements, even a hollow tree or log that you can crawl into for the night. You need to be aware that getting wet will not hurt you if you are warm, but the cold can kill you.

What kinds of shelters are the best and easiest? The old classic is the lean-to. It is quick and simple to build, and can be added onto as necessary. To build a lean-to, you need to find two forked sticks to act as uprights. You

Drawings of both a one–sided and two–sided lean–to.

drive the two stakes, forked sides up, into the ground and rest a pole between them. If you cannot find stakes with forks, you can use vines or grass or string to lash the pole to the sticks. Another way is to find two trees that are close together and rest a pole between the trees on their lower branches.

After the ridgepole is in place, you begin building a side by leaning sticks and branches against the pole at a forty-five degree angle. Once you have a sturdy side built, you can add insulation by piling on whatever material you can find: leaves, grass, branches, lichen, bark, or brush. A one-sided lean-to is fine if you are in a warm place in the summer. If the weather is cold, you should build another side (it looks like a pup tent) so that you are protected.

A lean-to is a great summer camping shelter. You can build a fire on the open side, sit back under the shelter protected from the elements, and enjoy the fire.

Another simple shelter is the tepee, or wickiup. To build the tepee, you need three long poles, six to eight

The two building stages of a tepee. You can also cover the poles with a tarp instead of vegetation, if you have one.

feet in length, that you lash together at one end. The ends that are not lashed, you stand upon the ground and spread into a tripod, creating a triangular inner space. You lean sticks and branches around the outside of the tepee until all but an entrance is covered.

The best protection from the cold is achieved by building a rib-hut. This is something like a lean-to, but one end of the ridgepole rests on the ground and the other on a tree stump or vertical stake driven into the ground. The ridgepole should be about ten to twelve feet long and very sturdy. The opening, the end resting on the tree stump or upright stake, should be only three or four feet off the ground at the most.

Next, you use sticks for ribs and stand them up along the ridgepole. These ribs should be at a steep angle, so that if it rains, the water will run off the shelter. After the ribs are in place, you begin piling on insulation material, just as with a lean-to. You keep piling on materials until the shelter is domed. The insulation over the ribs should be at least a foot or two thick.

Now you find more sticks and set up another row of ribs on each side of the pole to hold the insulating materials in place. Once this is done, you should try to find even more insulating material, and pile this on top of the second set of ribs. The more insulation, the more protection from the elements. In the mountains, you will find an abundance of materials to use in your shelter building.

Another simple shelter can be created by finding or digging a hollow in the ground large enough to hold you. Pile rocks up on three sides of the hole, and then fashion a roof across the rocks with sticks, grass, bark, and boughs. This is a good quick temporary shelter in dry weather. Remember to place the opening on the side away from the direction of the wind.

1. Tree stump or vertical stake in ground
2. Very sturdy Ridge Pole (10-12 ft. long)
   (Opening is 3-4 ft. off the ground)
3. First layer of Ribs: Sticks leaning @ vertical angle
4. First layer of Insulation
   (at least 1-2 ft thick)
5. Second layer of sticks
6. Second layer Insulation   RIB-HUT

A rib—hut. With its two layers of insulation, this is among the warmest of the survival shelters you can build.

Shelter is so important because it protects you from the wind, rain, snow, and sun. It also provides you with the comfort you need to sleep, which is vital for conserving your energy and staying mentally alert. Any of the shelters above can be built without tools, using materials found in all mountain wilderness areas.

The ground is often very cold at night, and you could lose body heat through it. It is a good idea to insulate the floor of your shelter for protection and comfort. Use whatever dry materials are available—for example, spruce tips or boughs—for a base. Cover this with grasses and leaves. If you have any spare clothing, you can pile that on top for added warmth. Make the bed springy and thick to protect you from the cold and shield you from the bumpy ground.

When I was learning about building shelters, my friends and I built a dome shelter in a field near our houses. The shelter lasted for several seasons with only a little cleaning and patching each year. Because of this, I think of a dome shelter as a kind of permanent shelter that you can build for long stays.

To build a small dome shelter, you need to find sixteen pliable sticks that are about two yards long. Draw a circle about two yards in diameter on the ground. You begin building by shoving one end of a stick on the circle line in the ground and a second stick directly opposite it on the other side of the circle. Next, you bend the tops of the two sticks to each other and tie them together with string. You repeat this process until all sixteen sticks are spaced equally around the perimeter.

The sticks form a circular dome. Decide where your entrance will be and then, working from the top down, weave pliable green branches through the frame in a circular fashion, working the small branches under and over the framing sticks. When all but the entrance is covered, you cover the woven branches with mud. If you don't want to use mud you don't have to, but it protects the inside from the wind and rain. However, it also makes the inside very dark. Use a flashlight inside for light.

Another kind of permanent shelter can be built by driving a line of stakes in the ground and then another line of stakes about a foot away from the first line. You dump

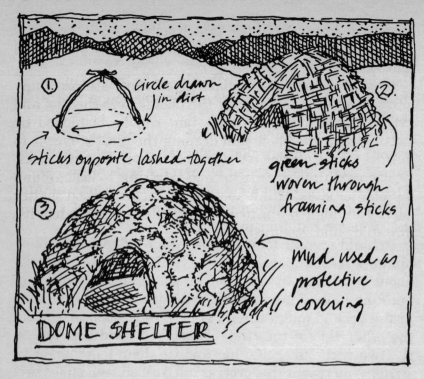

circle drawn in dirt

sticks opposite lashed together

green sticks woven through framing sticks

mud used as protective covering

DOME SHELTER

A homemade dome shelter. This can be made quite warm and permanent if you cover it with mud.

whatever branches and leaves and grass you can find between the two rows of stakes. This makes a well-insulated wall of natural materials. With this method, you can create walls to build whatever shape shelter you wish. The top is made of layers of branches.

Or you can make a kind of covering called thatch for any of these shelters by tying grasses together at one end and then tying the other end of the bundles of grass to the shelter. Thatching works best on angled roofs or tee-pees. With thatch, you always start at the bottom and work up, overlapping the thatch as you work your way toward the top of the shelter, the same way you would put shingles on a house.

If you have a piece of plastic, you can waterproof any of these shelters by placing the plastic over the roof and weighting it down. An easy tent can be fashioned by setting up a ridgepole and draping the plastic over it to form a tent. Hold down the ends of the plastic with rocks.

The next time you are hiking, take time to look around for shelter sites. Think about what makes a good shelter site. You might want to build a shelter from scratch; it's fun to do and good practice.

Chapter 5

The Essence of Life

Water is the essence of life. Without it we cannot live for long. Water makes up three-quarters of the human body. Our skins are sort of large liquid-holding containers. Water is vital to our physical well-being. Even if we don't take in water, we still continue to excrete liquid through sweat and urine.

You should always carry water when hiking, camping, or exploring in the mountains. In a survival situation, you may need to add to your water supply by collecting water from the environment. Water helps the body regulate body temperature and keeps it functioning properly.

If we don't drink enough water, we become dehydrated. Dehydration saps our strength and can cause nausea, confusion, poor muscle coordination, and many other problems. After three days without drinking any water, you can die of dehydration, and to stay in good shape you should never go longer than a day without liquids. Fortunately, in the mountains there are many ways of finding and collecting water.

This valuable liquid is more important than food. You can live for days, even weeks, without food if you have shelter and water. If you find yourself in a survival situation in the mountains, you should first find or build shelter. Then look for water.

At home you turn on the tap and out comes the clear, cool, life-giving substance. You don't think twice about drinking it; you believe it's safe because it has been treated, or because you have a well that has been tested and produces water that is drinkable. In the mountains, you must first find water and then make sure it is drinkable.

There are usually many sources of water. Streams, pools, springs, and small lakes or ponds are often found high in the mountains. Water runs down from the mountains to the river valleys.

The way to find water is to use common sense and observation skills. As you walk through the woods, listen for sounds of moving water. Listen for frogs. Look around and see if you can find places where water is likely to collect. Most grain-eating birds (such as finches), grazing animals, and flies are a sign that water is near. Look for animal paths. They will lead you to water.

If you don't find water right away, don't panic. There are ways of collecting water. Here is something to try in your back yard. Dig a hole about three feet deep and three or four feet in diameter (get your parents' permission first). Place a container in the bottom, the deepest part of the hole. Now, take a six-by-six-foot sheet of clear or milky plastic and cover the hole loosely with it. Secure the edges with dirt or rocks. Place a few rocks in the center of the plastic sheet to give it a funnel shape, but be careful not to puncture the plastic. You want the bottom of the plastic funnel pointing at the container beneath it in the bottom of the hole. You have just built a solar still.

A solar still will collect at least half a quart of water per day. This is enough to keep you alive. The important thing to remember is that you have to carry a sheet of plastic in your survival packet. This shouldn't be a problem, as plastic folds neatly into a small square and weighs very little.

The still works by creating a warm greenhouse effect under the plastic sheet. Water from the soil evaporates, causing droplets of condensation to form on the underside of the plastic sheet. The funnel shape of the plastic carries the water downward to the tip, where it drips into your container. Because your still is shaped like an upside-down umbrella, if it rains water will collect in the top, so be sure the sides of the plastic are well weighted.

It's a good idea to build a solar still in your backyard so that you will see how well it works. Once you are convinced, I think you will always carry a sheet of plastic in your survival kit.

If you are in a survival situation, be prepared to collect rainwater. Find bowl-shaped rocks and have them ready. If you have containers, leave them out at night in case it rains. Build a solar still and make sure the sides of the plastic sheet are well weighted. If you have nothing that holds water, you can make a wooden bowl by collecting red-hot coals from your camp fire and burning a bowl shape into a piece of dry wood. Remember that if you don't have water, and build a camp fire, you must always keep it under control and have something with which to smother the fire in an emergency.

In the mountains, you can collect dew very early in the morning. This is done by using a piece of cloth to wipe the moisture from plant and rock surfaces, then squeezing the moisture from the cloth into your mouth. This

A solar still used to collect fresh drinking water when there's no source of clean water available.

may sound like you would get very little moisture, but that is not the case. It is a lot of work, and you can only collect dew early in the morning, but it can keep you alive.

Rainwater, snow, ice, dew, and solar still water are all pure and need no treatment before drinking. Any other water should be purified before drinking. There are serious diseases you could catch from impure water, such as dysentery, cholera, and typhoid, and the water might also contain worms and leeches. If you are drinking water

Ways to Reduce Water Loss and Conserve Water

- Keep still to reduce sweating.
- Sip water rather than gulping. If you drink too fast when you are thirsty, it can make you sick.
- If it is summer, and very hot, keep to the shade. If work needs to be done around your camp, work in the morning but avoid working during the midday.
- Eat little. Water is needed for digestion.
- Travel when it is cool.
- This sounds awful, but in a real emergency, urine can be drunk if first purified in a solar still.
- Don't use valuable water to brew coffee or tea. Both dehydrate you.

from a stream, the nearer you are to the source the better. Usually, the higher up the mountain, the safer the water. Standing water can collect bacteria. Any water other than those listed above as safe should be purified.

There are two ways to purify water. Boiling water for fifteen minutes is one way. The other is to use chlorine tablets, available in sporting goods stores and often at your pharmacy.

If you don't have chlorine tablets and you have collected your water in a burned-out wooden collection bowl, it can still be purified. The way to do this is to heat rocks in your fire and drop them into the water. It will take a few rocks to get the water up to boiling, but once the water is hot it will boil easily.

When you are in the mountains, you should make it a habit to notice water sources. This habit will make it easy for you to find water in a survival situation because you will learn to recognize the ways of water in the mountains. When you see water ask yourself if it's drinkable. Is the water moving fast? How near is the source? Are there signs of plant and animal life around? Does the water look clear, or are there signs of stagnation?

Plants can be sources of water as well. Wild grapes and crab apples both have significant amounts of moisture in them. You can eat the stalks of bull thistle. After re-

How Much Water Do You Need?

The chart below tells you how much water you need every day if you are resting in the shade. If you are moving around, or out in the full sun, you need more.

Temperature	Water Needed Per Day
68° F	1.8 pints
77° F	2.1 pints
86° F	4.4 pints
95° F	8.8 pints

Remember, a pint is sixteen ounces.

moving the top thistle and peeling, you'll find that the young stalks contain a fair amount of moisture.

On Mt. San Gorgonio, I ate snow because I was thirsty. This is something you should not do. It takes calories— energy—to melt the snow when you eat it. The same is true of ice. If you are trying to keep up your strength, it is best to melt the snow and even let the water warm up a little before drinking it.

If possible, you should drink plenty of water when you are in the mountains. At higher altitudes, people often do not know that they are becoming dehydrated. So even if it is not a survival situation, make it a habit to drink several glasses of water every day.

Chapter 6

Fire in the Mountains

You can survive without fire, but it would be very difficult. A well-built fire is one that is just big enough to satisfy your needs. If the fire is too large it wastes fuel. A fire should be just big enough to cook over, or warm you, or tell stories around. A fire that is not too large is easier to manage and less trouble to put out when you leave.

Besides the three uses for fire mentioned above, fire provides light and sterilizes water. Its warmth can be used for treating hypothermia, drying clothes, and even thawing frozen boots. There is a notion that animals are afraid of camp fire, but I think that this is learned. Camp fires keep animals away because the creatures know that humans are with the fire.

The ancient Greeks believed that one of their gods, Prometheus, gave fire to humans to set them above the animals. In every culture there are legends of how fire was discovered. The flames of a fire are not only beautiful, but in many cultures the children look for shapes in the flames and make up stories. In the woods, in the mountains, late at night, when it is very dark, the light from the fire is comforting. It keeps real and imaginary creatures away.

While the uses of fire are many, you must not forget that it must be respected. *Fire can be very dangerous.* If you have ever accidentally burned yourself, you know how true this is.

Before lighting a fire, you must be sure to choose a location that is safe. There should be no objects nearby, such as overhanging branches, that might catch fire. The area around where the fire is to be built should be cleared of dead leaves and dried twigs or branches. If it is windy, a protective ring should be constructed around the fire site by digging a shallow pit and placing stones around the edge in a circle. The fire should not be closer to your shelter than six feet.

If it is very cold, you can use rocks to build a curved wall on one side of the fire. This acts as a reflector for the heat and light of the flames. Rocks can also be heated near the fire to place in your sleeping bag as bed warmers. (Make sure they are cool enough to hold in your hands or they may burn your bag!) If you heat rocks, you should make sure that they are not from a stream bed. Once a rock exploded when I was heating it. This was because the rock had moisture trapped inside which expanded when it was heated. If you heat rocks, it is best to collect them from the south side of a mountain where the sun has dried them.

After you have cleared a site and made sure it is a safe spot for your fire, you will need to collect materials to burn. You will need tinder, kindling, and firewood. For tinder, small dry pieces of grass, bark, or dry fibrous stalks work well. They all catch fire quickly. The purpose of tinder is to hold a flame briefly, until the kindling catches the flame. Small bits of paper make an excellent tinder, too. For kindling, dry twigs and pieces of wood that are about as big around as a pencil are good. And for firewood, any dry branches or sticks that are a half-inch around or larger are good. Once the fire is going, you can add bigger pieces of wood.

Here are some things I have learned that might be helpful:

- If you're gathering kindling and you are not sure if a branch or twig is dry enough to build your fire, break it. If it breaks with a snap, then it is good dry wood.

- If it is raining, look for dry wood under standing trees. Often you will be able to find lower branches that are dead. This is true of bushes as well. It is very difficult to build a fire in the rain unless you can find some sort of safe shelter, such as an over-hanging rock, to protect the fire.

- Finally, if you can't find rocks to use as a windbreak, larger pieces of green wood can be placed around the fire to dry and then be added to the fire.

The best camping fire is shaped like a tepee. When your fire ring is ready, place a small amount of tinder and kindling in the middle of the circle. Using other pieces of kindling like pick-up-sticks, build a small tepee around the tinder and kindling, leaning the pencil-sized sticks against each other in a circle. Leave one side of the tepee open to light the tinder. A fire needs oxygen to burn, so the tepee should be a loose little bundle of kindling around the burning materials. Next, stand the larger pieces of wood around the kindling to form an outer tepee.

"TEPEE" FIRE

A "tepee fire," so named because of its resemblance to the frame of a tepee.

Now, strike a match and light the tinder. The flame will glow as it spreads through the tinder. Then the kindling will start to catch, and after a while the outer wood will reach 452° Fahrenheit and burn. Don't add new fuel too quickly. Let the fire burn for a while. The tepee will collapse as it burns, and new wood should be added when the fire is glowing red with coals.

It is easiest to start a fire with a match or lighter. There are other ways to light a fire, but a match or lighter is easiest, and you should not be without one or the other if you plan an extended trip in the mountains.

The best way to keep matches dry when you are hiking in the mountains is to keep them in a small plastic container. Thirty-five millimeter film comes in a plastic container perfect for this purpose. In fact, these small film containers are good for all sorts of little kits—sewing, first aid, fishing, etc.—and collections of things you find while hiking. If you don't know anyone with a camera, a photo store that processes film will often give you these containers.

Since this book is about being safe in the mountains, you should know other ways to start a fire. The next simplest way is to use a piece of steel, such as a knife blade, and flint. When steel comes in contact with flint it sparks. Sporting goods stores sell "sparkers" which are used to light gas stoves. These metal fire starters work on the same principle as those plastic spark guns they sell in toy stores, and are really just a piece of steel that scrapes against a pad of flint. A lighter works on the same principle, only the spark lights a gas or fluid fuel. The problem with this method is that you must carry a knife or piece of steel and be able to identify and find rocks which contain flint. There is a another problem: getting tinder to ignite from a spark is very difficult. The pioneers used this method, but they had a great deal of patience and perseverance. I have tried several times to start a fire this way without success.

I discovered that some sporting goods stores sell small blocks of magnesium—a soft metal that ignites easily—for use in lighting fires. It's a kind of backup fire starter that lights even when wet and doesn't require special treatment to store. You shave a few strips of magnesium onto your tinder and a spark will ignite it instantly.

Another way to start a fire is by using a magnifying glass or lens to focus the sun's rays on the tinder—the solar method. This method doesn't work on overcast days, and becomes more and more difficult after midday. To start a fire this way requires that you carry a magnifying lens when you go hiking or camping. You might find distorted pieces of ordinary glass that will work, but it is easier just to carry a magnifying lens. A camera lens will work as well. Experiment with this method, but make sure you have your parents' permission.

The most difficult fire-starting method relies on friction and elbow grease. It is probably the oldest method known to man for starting a fire. Mastering this technique requires effort and patience, but once you learn to start a fire using only natural materials, you will feel a new confidence. The Bow Method requires four pieces of wood. Each of these four pieces of wood has a name: the fireboard, the handhold, the bow, and the spindle.

The spindle and fireboard are best made of dry wood of about the same hardness. The handhold is best made of harder wood or a rock or piece of bone. The bow should be made from a sturdy, curved branch that is either green or seasoned but not rotten.

Here's how it works. The spindle is a short (about eight or nine inches) cylinder. It is best to whittle one end round and the other end pointed. The round end will fit into your handhold and the pointed end into the fireboard. The fireboard should be about a half-inch thick and long enough for you to hold down with your foot while drilling the spindle. You must carve out a depression in the fireboard that will hold the pointed end of the spindle.

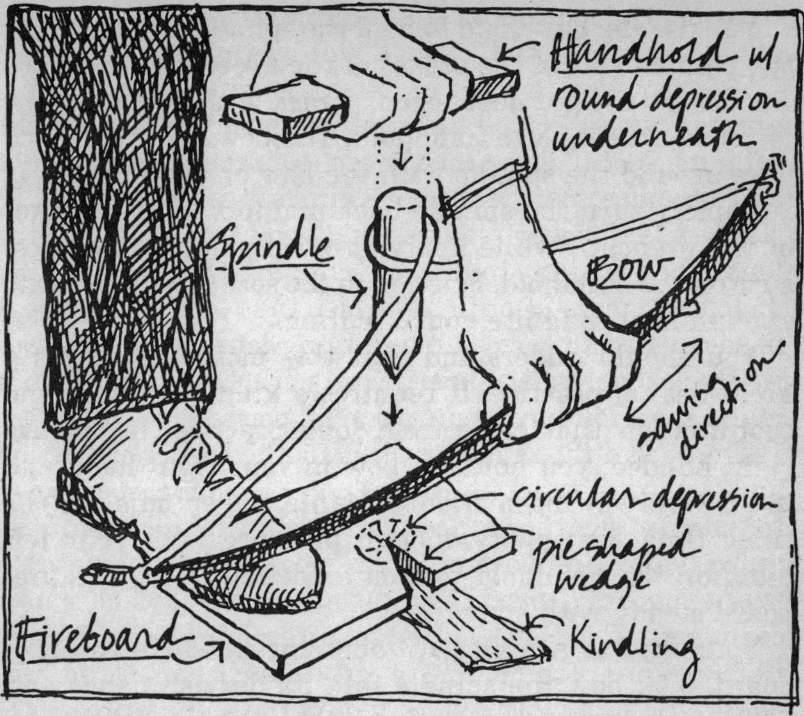
Handhold w/ round depression underneath
Spindle
Bow
sawing direction
circular depression
pie shaped wedge
Fireboard
Kindling

The "bow method" of fire starting. Make sure that the kindling you use is dry, and that you work right next to where your fire is built.

Once you have shaped the ends of the spindle and shaved the circular socket into the fireboard, you are almost ready to begin. But first, you have to cut a thin pie-shaped wedge from the edge of your fireboard to almost the center of the socket. (See illustration.)

Now, string your bow—you can use a shoelace, vine, or strong piece of string or rope—by tying a strong permanent knot on one end and an adjustable knot on the other end. (Read about knots in Chapter 10.)

You use the handhold to hold the spindle upright, with the pointed end in the socket of the fireboard. Any hard wood with a slight depression or rock with a scoop shape is good for using as a handhold. The bowstring is looped once around the spindle with the bow on the outside.

Rapidly turn the spindle back and forth in the socket of the fireboard while applying steady downward pressure on the handhold. Friction in the socket will generate enough heat to ignite your kindling.

You should understand that this method requires a great deal of practice. It requires a kind of rhythm and coordination that come from long practice. If you are right-handed, you hold the bow in your right hand and use a level sawing motion to rotate the spindle. At the same time, you apply enough pressure with your left hand on the handhold to create friction. Keep the fireboard steady with your foot.

Your kindling is placed under the notch in the fireboard. You bow the spindle into its dervish dance and work with a smooth, steady motion. After a while you will notice smoke from the socket. When this happens, keep on drilling the spindle into the fireboard until there is a great deal of smoke. When you see little red particles of glowing red-hot dust falling into the notch, you should stop bowing and lift the fireboard gently over the kindling. A small hot coal should drop into the tinder from the fireboard socket. You must work quickly to see that the tinder ignites. Blow on it gently until it reddens and begins to glow. Keep blowing until it ignites. There, your first fire from all-natural materials!

It took me more than a month to learn to build a fire using this method. While satisfying, it requires a great deal of practice, and if you can get help from a woodsman, father, mother, or scout leader, the learning goes much faster. You want your helper to watch your form and make sure you are holding the spindle upright and bowing evenly.

If you use green wood, you will never light a fire using this method, so be careful and select dry wood for the spindle and fireboard. Another helpful tip is to add some grease to the handhold where the top of the spindle fits into the holder. This allows the spindle to turn faster without generating too much heat on the handhold. Remember, this is a friction method of fire-starting. If you are in the woods and need something to lubricate the handhold but don't have any fat or grease, you can rub your finger along the crease of the side your nose where body oils accumulate and then rub the oil on your handhold.

If the spindle wobbles too much as you drill, use your bent leg as a brace to steady your arm. This is one method where it is best to remember that practice makes perfect.

Now that you know how to build a fire, you should be aware of the rules for preventing forest fires:

1) **Never light a fire or strike a match without a purpose.**
2) **Never throw a lighted match to the ground.**
3) **Never leave a fire or camping stove unattended.**
4) **When you break camp, make sure the fire is completely dead.**

If you are ever caught in a forest fire, you should check which way the wind is blowing. If the wind is blowing in the direction of the fire, away from you, head *into* the wind and try to find a gap in the trees, or a river, for protection.

If the wind is blowing toward you, you will have to get a move on, as fires can travel fast. Try to get around the fire, but if it catches up with you, look for a deep gully or ditch and take refuge. You should never move up the side of the mountain, as fire travels faster when going uphill.

You probably know all the safety rules—but bear with me a moment while I give them to you once more.

- When building a fire, make sure that the location is far enough away from trees, bushes, and vegetation that might catch fire.
- Make sure your equipment and clothing are out of the way.
- Do not leave your fire unattended. If you have chores that will take you away from your fire, do them before starting the fire.
- Have water and a blanket handy in case the fire should get out of control.
- And remember, don't build a fire larger than you will need for heat, warmth, and light, for cooking, and for stories.

Chapter 7

Dining Out

Climbing a mountain is sort of like starting out in the dense Canadian forests and walking to the North Pole. What I mean by this is that as you work your way higher up the mountain, plants and animals become more scarce. At the base of a mountain you might find meadows with a variety of grasses and insects. As you move higher, the meadows will give way to woods where maple, wild apple, oak, walnut, beech, and other leafy trees flourish. A little higher up, the leaf-bearing trees give way to the evergreens. Eventually even the evergreens become thinner and give way to rock, where lichens and tiny alpine flowers color the treeless landscape above the timberline. At the very top, if the mountain is very tall, you will find snow and ice.

Common sense will tell you that you will have a hard time finding food or shelter above the timberline (at around ten thousand feet). The abundance of berries, wild apples, acorns, and other edible plants that people often describe in survival books is lower down the mountain near the base.

The good news is that if you are lost in the mountains, food is not the most important survival item. In fact, you can survive for up to a month without food as long as you are protected from the elements and have water. It would not be pleasant to go without food for thirty days, and it could cause physical problems, but it is possible.

There are some plants and (ugh) bugs that you can eat in an emergency. It is important to be able to identify these plants, shrubs, trees, bugs, whatever. Go on a nature walk with someone who knows about plants and ask questions. Many books give descriptions and pictures of the plants. But there is no substitute for learning to identify the plants in the field. Besides, it's fun.

There are many poisonous plants, so *do not experiment*. Even if you see an animal eating a plant it does not mean that the plant is safe for humans. Trapping animals for food is possible, but with proper preparedness it is a situation you should never find yourself in. There is a danger in trapping animals, too. A trapped animal, even a very small trapped animal, is a dangerous animal. You run the risk of being badly bitten.

Never eat wild mushrooms.

Never eat red berries.

Just about every variety of bladed grass can be eaten. This includes meadow grasses as well as the cereal grasses such as wheat and oats. Eating grass may sound unpleasant, but grass is a rich source of vitamins and minerals. You can get the nutrients from grass the way that many animals do, by chewing the grass and then spitting it out.

Oak trees are pretty common, and you can eat the acorns if you boil them for several hours. The boiling reduces the bitter taste. The problem for mountain climbers is that you will only find oak trees at the lower elevations and preparing acorns to eat is a pain. But knowing that you can eat them is, maybe, comforting.

The mainstay food of survival books is cattails. I've never had them. Experts say you can eat every part of the cattail, and some people even think they are pretty tasty. But again, you don't usually find cattails in the mountains. You find them in marshy, wet ground and swampy areas. Once, in the Green Mountains of Vermont, I found a small wet area about a third of the way up the side of a mountain, and there were cattails growing at the edge of this mountain pond. But as you go higher up, they will be harder to find.

Birds love wild berries and often plant berry patches for us. You can find wild berries, such as raspberries and blackberries, growing on the lower slopes of mountains. Their sweet pulpy fruit is fun to eat and tastes delicious. But higher up the mountain you will not find berries.

Pine trees are tall, with rough scaly bark, and have sharp evergreen needles which are arranged in bundles of two to five. Female pine trees have pine cones which look like many-petaled eggs. Underneath each of these "petals" are a couple of seeds. You can identify the seeds because they have wings.

Pine needles are a good source of vitamin C, but you don't eat them, though. You chop them up and make a tea and drink the tea. The seeds can be eaten if you heat the winged pod until it splits.

There are many other common edible plants that you often find on the lower regions of a mountain. Just a few of them are:

- BLACKBERRIES—These are juicy red or black berries that are found on thorny vines. The vines grow in thickets, so they look bushy. The berries are de-

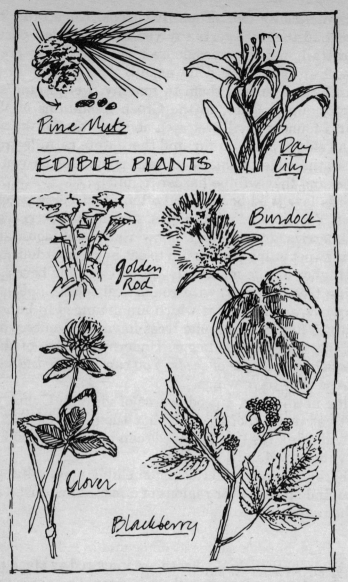

Pine Nuts

EDIBLE PLANTS

Day Lily

Burdock

Golden Rod

Clover

Blackberry

Some common edible plants. Be sure to double check any plant in an identification book before consuming it.

licious, and you can also use the leaves to make black-berry tea. But watch out for those thorns; they can hurt.

- BURDOCK—This is a troublesome weed that grows throughout North America, Canada, and Hawaii. You have probably encountered burdock without knowing it. The seed of this weed is the stubborn burr that snags you when you are pathfinding. It's the burr that seems impossible to get out of your socks. Before this plant goes to seed, the root is edible. In fact, in Hawaii a domestic version of burdock is grown and the chopped-up root is used in many dishes. When the plant is young, the leaves are broad and only a few inches off the ground. The root is long and deep, and more often than not, has to be dug out of the ground. To eat the root you should peel it and boil it like a vegetable. The leaves can be eaten if you boil them and then change the water and boil them again.

- CLOVER—You probably don't need help in identifying clover. This plant is found in just about every area in the United States. It grows to a maximum height of about eighteen inches. The flower can be boiled to make a tea, and the leaves of the young plant can be eaten raw.

- DANDELION—This is another common plant which most everyone can identify. You can eat the stems, leaves, flowers and root of this plant. Many people eat dandelions in salads at home and in restaurants.

- GOLDENROD—It smells like licorice, and has long, unnotched leaves. It gets its name from the tiny yellow flower heads that cluster in cylindrical beauty on one side of the plant. Goldenrod is found in the central and eastern U.S.A. You can boil the leaves and eat them, and use the flowers to make tea.

- ROSES—These not only smell good; you can eat them. The petals can be eaten right from the bush, or you can use them to make a tea.
- SUNFLOWER—This plant grows three to twelve feet tall on rough thick stems. The flower heads, from three to eight inches across, contain the seeds in a neat disk-like cluster framed by large yellow flower petals. You can eat the seeds raw.
- DAYLILY—You can fry the flower buds. You can also eat the tubers (roots) by peeling them and boiling them like potatoes.

Other foods that taste good and can be found in and around the mountains are wild apples and grapes. Be ready for a surprise if you find wild grapes. They are not as sweet and juicy as the kind you find in the super-market.

Now for the yucky part. Probably the easiest source of food you will find in the mountains is earthworms. They are not found above the timberline, but as you head down the mountain they become more plentiful. You can fry them, boil them, or eat them raw (ugh). The same is true of maggots and slugs.

If you don't have the stomach for worms, and there is water nearby, you can use them as bait and fish for your dinner. Another creature that you will find around water is the bullfrog. While this creature may not sound like something good to eat, in some parts of the world the hind legs of the frog are considered delicacies. To hunt frogs you will need to use a net or a slingshot. They are

Poisonous Plants

Never eat any nuts, berries, roots, leaves, or flowers unless you *know* that they are edible. Because an animal eats a plant does not mean it is okay for you to eat it. The animal may not be affected by the poisons, but humans would be.

Never eat any mushrooms or toadstools in the wild.

Never eat red berries—they are usually poisonous.

Learn to identify plants poisonous to the touch:

- Poison ivy
- Poison sumac
- Poison oak

The following are DEADLY poisonous plants when eaten:

- Holly—Poisonous berries.
- Yew—Poisonous leaves and berries.
- Deadly nightshade—Poisonous berries.
- Laburnum—All parts are poisonous.
- Hemlock—All parts are poisonous.
- Foxglove—All parts are poisonous.

easiest to catch at night when they are singing. You will need a flashlight for your hunting. But with all living creatures, you should not trap and kill them unless it is absolutely necessary, and you should have the training

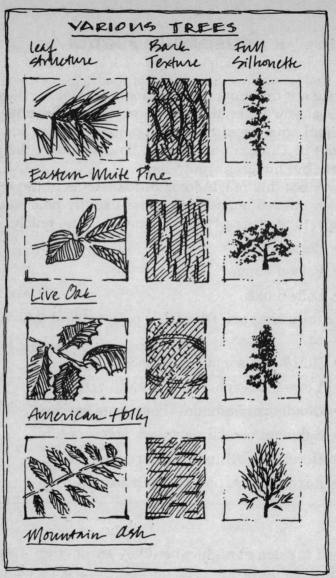

VARIOUS TREES

Leaf Structure	Bark Texture	Full Silhouette

Eastern White Pine

Live Oak

American Holly

Mountain Ash

Some trees described in the text. Use shape, bark and leaf formation to help identify a tree correctly.

and skills for this. A hunting skills class or a hunting trip with your family may teach you this.

There is a book called *Stalking the Wild Asparagus,* by Euell Gibbons, which is loaded with suggestions for finding and preparing natural wild foods. Many good field guides to flowers, trees, plants, and herbs are also available at your local library or bookstore. Your local nature museum or Audubon Society will often sponsor nature

A Tree Can Be

A musical instrument:	A violin is usually made from spruce or maple.
	A guitar is usually made from spruce or maple.
	A piano is often made of maple.
Sporting equipment:	A baseball bat is made of ash.
	So is a tennis racket.
	Skis are often a complex mixture of laminated plastics metal, but you will often find a heart of ash.
	Because it resists rot, spruce is used for building boats.

A Tree Can Be

School equipment: Your pencil is made of
                               cedar.

                               Desks are often oak.

Other things made of   Toys are made of oak,
wood: birch, ash, and pine.

                               Furniture is made from
                               a variety of woods in-
                               cluding sycamore, ce-
                               dar, maple, oak, pine
                               and cherry.

                               If you live in a wooden
                               house, it is a combina-
                               tion of oak, fir, and
                               pine.

Look around and see if you can identify the different types
of wood used to build the everyday things we find around
us.

Chapter 8

Moving Life

Animals are always surprising. In the wild, they are the ultimate survivalists, having to cope with an ever-changing environment. The inhabitants of the mountainous areas of the world are as varied as the mountains on which they live, for many reasons. The two most obvious reasons are food and safety. The competition for food in the lowlands is so great that they have been forced to head for the hills. Although they do contain many predators, there are less in mountain regions than in low regions.

Animals have learned to survive in the varied conditions imposed by the mountains: wind, cold, ice, snow, limited food supplies, and oxygen-thin air. They move about on a terrain that is rocky and steep, where the footing is less than ideal. Like humans, they require food, drink, and shelter.

The biggest in size of the mountain inhabitants are the deer, elk, bighorn sheep, rocky mountain goat, and black or brown bear. Bears are omnivores; they eat both plants and meat; all the others are herbivores, eating plants only.

Foxes, coyotes, and mountain lions are predators. That means they hunt, kill, and eat other animals. While the fox and coyote live off smaller game such as rabbits, rodents, or squirrels, the mountain lion's primary target is deer.

The mountain lion is known by many names: puma, catamount, panther, or cougar. It is the largest carnivore (meat eater) common to North America. By hunting deer, the mountain lion is a natural controller of herd size. If the deer population becomes too great, they overgraze the forest, causing damage.

Mountain lions are actually not dangerous to man. There is one reported occasion on which a mountain lion killed and ate a thirteen-year-old Washington State boy in 1924, but this incident is the exception, not the rule. Mountain lions are curious and may follow you in the woods, but they will leave you alone.

Bears have been reported to attack humans on several occasions. When I was fifteen, I went on a hike in the high, bear-inhabited mountains of Glacier International Park in northern Montana. Having heard stories about bears attacking hikers, I was a little concerned about the safety of this outing. Then I met a park ranger who told me the secret of remaining safe from bears.

"Bears will only attack a human if startled," he told me, "The secret is to let them know you're coming."

The park ranger gave me a small bell to tie to my shoelaces. My hike was made more pleasant by the reassuring musical jingle which accompanied my walk. Other people sing or whistle as they hike, and keeping a conversation running if you are not alone works, too.

The smaller animals of the mountains are herbivores and include rabbits, squirrels, and marmots. Rodents, such as the mountain shrew and meadow vole, provide year-round food for the foxes, coyotes, hawks, and weasels.

Rodents are the most common mountain mammals; they remain active throughout the year. They survive the winter by building warm nests under the snow. The rodents breed so quickly they would exterminate themselves by overpopulation and resulting starvation if they were not the food staple of so many animals.

When winter comes to the mountains, the animals react in different ways. The larger herbivores—deer, elk, goats, and sheep—migrate to lower feeding grounds, and the predators follow. The rodents build nests and remain active throughout the winter. Hibernation is the way many other small animals deal with extreme cold. The bear is the only large animal that hibernates. The ground squirrel's behavior is a good way to show how hibernation works. The squirrel eats and eats during the summer and autumn months, until it becomes heavy with stored fat. When winter arrives, the squirrel gets comfortable in its burrow and goes to sleep until winter is over. But this is not a normal sleep, because the body temperature drops to about fifty degrees. The squirrel's heartbeat drops from the normal two hundred beats per minute to a mere twenty. Come spring, the squirrel wakes up feeling thin and good.

Hibernation is a way of protecting animals from the extreme cold. It slows down body functions to almost non-existence. Some animals become dormant, or torpid, only if exposed to extreme cold. One winter I forgot to turn on the heat in the room where I had a pet hamster. When I came home I found him curled in a ball, cold, and without a heartbeat that I could detect.

Knowing that some animals become torpid in the winter, I placed the hamster on a heating pad to warm him slowly. After about half an hour his leg twitched. I gave him a few drops of sugar water from an eyedropper, and within the hour he was eating Cheerios. The hamster's hibernation was a way of protecting himself from freezing to death. By the way, I don't recommend you try chilling your hamster to see it hibernate.

(There is a process called aestivation in which animals are dormant during the hot summer months. This happens with some desert creatures.)

Another group of animals found in the mountains are insects. They probably have been carried to the mountains by the winds. Insects are a food source for birds. The mosquito is the most irritating. Its bite may itch for several days. Camp fire smoke, citronella candles, and commercial insect repellents are all effective in keeping mosquitoes away from you. Spiders and bees will leave you alone unless you step on them or surprise them in some other way.

In the northeastern U.S., you have to watch out for the deer tick. Ticks range from the size of a grain of pepper to the size of a watermelon seed. They are attracted to warm-blooded animals—dogs, cats, horses, cows, deer, humans, etc.—and attach themselves to their prey with bow-shaped pincers that are located on either side of their heads. They live off of the warm, rich blood of the animals.

The deer tick is one of the smaller ticks, the size of a tiny freckle. Some deer ticks transmit a disease known as Lyme Disease, so called because it was discovered in Lyme, Connecticut. This disease causes headaches, stiffness in the joints, and, in some cases, a circular rash around the bite area.

Some animals that you might see on a hike into the mountains.

Lyme Disease is treatable. The problem is, there is no way yet of knowing if a tick is carrying the disease. If you are bitten, you won't probably know whether you have it until symptoms develop. Not all deer ticks carry Lyme Disease. You can call the local health department to find out if cases have been reported in your area. Remember, this is currently only a problem in the Northeast, but it may spread to other areas.

You must be careful, when removing ticks, to remove the head and pincers. This is best done by using tweezers, but you can use your fingers. Because of Lyme Disease, companies are making tick repellent sprays, but it's uncertain if they work or if you should use them. Check with your own doctor if you're concerned.

Snakes are also found lower on mountains. The majority of snakes are nonpoisonous, but you should know which snakes are poisonous and how to treat a snake bite. Snake bite kits are available in sporting goods stores. If you are bitten by a snake that *is* poisonous, you should act quickly. First, tie a piece of cloth or rope around your leg or arm, between the bite and your heart (almost all snake bites are on the legs of victims). This slows the circulation of the poison in your system. Then use a sharp knife or razor, which should be sterilized, if possible, to make an X-shaped cut over the bite and use suction to remove as much poison as possible. Snake bite kits have little suction cups designed for this purpose. Most important, get medical attention.

One of the pleasures of exploring the mountains is observing animals or their signs. Two items that are good to carry on day trips are a lightweight pair of binoculars and a small bag of plaster of paris. The best way to observe animals is to find a spot near an animal trail or near where they drink and sit quietly. You can wait for the animals to come to you.

What's the plaster of paris for? It hardens fast, within a few minutes, making it excellent for collecting animal footprints. A clean print makes an excellent mold for the plaster.

The plants and animals of the mountains are worth studying. If you spent every day observing them, your education would be endless. A very good book about collecting and studying plants and animals is *The Amateur Naturalist*, by Gerald Durrell.

Chapter 9

Survival Hunting

In a recent popular movie, a scene stands out in my mind: A man in the Australian outback offers a beautiful journalist grubs as a survival food. In the sequel, the same man is in New York City, where he demonstrates his rock-throwing skills for a group of children.

Why do these scenes stand out? The first scene was so gross that I don't think anyone would forget it. But it also reminds us that we are part of the food chain. Like bears, we are omnivores. We eat both animals and plants. For Aborigines in some parts of Australia, grubs are part of their diet. If they didn't eat them they wouldn't survive.

The second scene is memorable because it shows the degree of skill necessary for survival hunting. I'm not sure the actor in the film could really hit a tin can with a rock at twenty or thirty feet, but people who count on their skills to survive become very good at their own particular way of hunting. Survival hunting involves using your wits to catch animals.

All hunting should be for survival purposes only. You should never kill an animal or damage a plant just for fun. It is fine to go out on a plant walk and identify and sample plants. Learning to identify plants in their environment is one of the most satisfying pleasures you will experience. Knowledge expands your world.

Taking the life of an animal is an experience you will not forget. It is a serious undertaking, and should be done with the knowledge that the animal is giving its life for you. To hunt, you should learn to understand and respect the animals you are hunting. And the key word here is *learn*. If you plan on hunting, you should learn and know all the skills necessary and required by law. In some parts of the country there may be junior hunting skills classes, or perhaps you will learn these skills in Scouts.

At one time, hunting was considered a part of growing up in our culture. Parents taught their children how to harvest plants and hunt animals for food. During the American pioneer period, hunting was the way meat was put on the table. Theodore Roosevelt wrote a book about teaching his son to hunt.

Today, most of us shop for meat in the supermarket and buy our edible plants there as well. But there are still people growing and harvesting those plants, and there are still people raising and killing animals for our survival. The process has just become simpler, one step removed. Our hunting is done in the supermarket and money is our weapon. Our lifestyle has taken us away from the hunting grounds.

Many people have mixed feelings about hunting. Some believe that we should not kill and eat animals. These people have chosen to eat only plants. That is fine. You can survive in the mountains without hunting animals for food.

Other people believe that hunting is not wrong. These people do not think of hunting as a process in which animals are killed for fun. They believe hunters are serious nature lovers who understand and care about the wilderness environment. Some say hunting is in our blood, that it goes back to a primitive survival instinct passed down to us from our ancestors. Hunting is a way to be a part of nature in a real sense, to depend upon the animals we kill for our own lives. In this way, only do we feel that we are part of the mountain wilderness, but also we understand our place in this environment. In order to hunt, we must know the habitat and ways of the animals we are eating.

In the sense that hunting is about understanding the ways of the animal and its habitat, then hunting is about getting back to our ancestral environment. Going to the mountains is about getting back to the smell of growing things, testing ourselves against the elements, about the sun on our faces and the mystery of survival, of life.

And death.

Killing an animal will change you. You should discuss hunting with your parents. In Virginia, where I lived at one time, fox hunting was a regular occurrence. On their first fox hunt, young people were smeared with the blood of the newly-killed fox as a sign of initiation into adulthood. In a very good film about hunting in Africa, called *In The Blood,* the same ritual takes place when a young man makes his first kill. The point is that killing an animal is such a powerful event that it is seen as an initiation into adulthood.

In this chapter I'm going to tell you about survival hunting. You probably already know something about fishing, but I'll show you how to make a fish trap and a couple of basic animal traps as well. Again, keep in mind that a trapped animal can be dangerous.

There are many edible animals and insects in the

mountains. You can eat any kind of fish. Remember, we are talking about in the mountains. It is not true that you can eat all fish elsewhere. A few fish are actually poisonous. Many others may be contaminated with poisons from factory or farm runoff or sewage. You can eat reptiles, birds, and mammals. Birds are the most difficult to trap. Grasshoppers and crickets and worms can keep you healthy, but you should cook them first. I've already mentioned frogs in the last chapter. You should not eat furry caterpillars—I doubt that you would have much of a desire to anyway!—as they may be poisonous.

In a book I read, a man used fishing lines with worms attached to catch birds. This seems like a lot of work for such a small meal. If there is water anywhere near, you would be better off using your worms and hooks to catch fish. But if you spot a bird's nest, check it for eggs. A nesting bird will keep laying eggs if you take only a few of the eggs. This way, you can go back each day and take the fresh eggs.

Fishing is a good way to put dinner on the table in a survival situation. In your survival kit you should have a few hooks and some fishing line. A branch makes a good pole, and a few worms or insects provide the bait. But if you're caught without fishing line or hooks, you can still catch fish.

Using sticks to form a V-shaped wall, with a bowl at the bottom of the V, in a narrow part of a stream bed will create a barrier that traps fish. You can catch the fish in the bowl with a sharp stick or net.

Another method is to make a kind of basket net out of young green saplings and place it in the stream current.

Warning: These are illegal ways of catching fish. Do not try them unless you are in a survival situation.

In hunting animals, you should learn their habits and behaviors. The best way to do this is spend time watching animals when you are in the mountains. What I mean by watching animals is to look with purpose. Learn to identify animal tracks. Keep a watch for squirrels and chipmunks and deer. Listen. Can you identify bird songs or hear water in the distance? Stop from time to time and just look around. Keep in mind that animals have need of shelter, water, and food.

Another way to learn about animals is to spend time in the library. There are numerous books on animals, as well as books on nature, plants, hunting, and fishing. Learn each time you go to the library and each time you walk up a mountain.

Why learn about animal habits? In a survival situation, you need to have some idea of an animal's habits to set a trap.

Remember—these traps are illegal and should only be used in survival situations.

These traps do not determine the animal they will catch. Do not set one up and leave it in your backyard, as you could kill or harm a pet. Treat all aspects of hunting with respect.

Most animals have excellent senses of smell and sight. For this reason, you must take extra care in hiding your trap and making sure it does not have your scent. Traps can be camouflaged by using natural materials you find in the woods, such as leaves or grass. The wood used in building traps should be strong and light, and any parts that you carve from it should be rubbed with dirt or ashes to darken the exposed wood. To take the scent off wood that you have handled, or to cover the scent, rub the wood with plant leaves or ashes.

The Figure 4 deadfall trap is easy to build. You can practice using it by substituting a shoe box, or other cardboard box, for the weight. A deadfall trap works by tricking an animal into triggering the release mechanism, and when that happens a weight drops, trapping the animal.

Some things about using a deadfall should be clear at once. The weight that drops on the animal should be heavy enough to kill it, but not so heavy that it flattens the creature. The purpose is catching food. If the weight is too light, the injured animal might get away and die in the woods.

This kind of trap requires bait. Different animals prefer different types of bait. The best animal to trap is the rabbit: since it is a herbivore, you can use plants as bait. There are two kinds of human food that most animals and fish are attracted to: cheese and peanut butter. Cheese is an excellent fishing bait.

The size of the animal you are trapping should determine the size of your trap and the type of bait. Since the weight is dropping onto the animal, it would be difficult to build a deadfall to trap a deer. Using cheese for bait and a shoe box, you might want to experiment with using a deadfall to catch mice. The box should be heavy enough so that the mouse cannot escape or chew through it right away.

This brings up another point—many animals search for food at night. The advantage of a trap is that you can check it each morning. Anyway, your chances of catching something are improved if the animal does not smell your scent in the area. (You can rub the inside of birch bark on your skin to prevent animals from smelling you.)

To build a deadfall you need bait, three sticks and a

weight. The method is simple. A central stick, with a Y at the top and a flat ledge cut out about halfway between the ground and the Y, is driven into the ground. A cross stick, with a notch cut at a right angle, is held in place by the weight of the deadfall. The cross stick acts as bait holder and trigger. One end of the cross stick is pointed to hold the bait and the other end is notched to support the angled weight-holding stick.

The angled stick supports the weight of the deadfall. One end holds the weight and the other end is tapered to fit into the notch on the cross stick. This kind of deadfall is called a Figure 4 because the three sticks look like a 4 when the trap is assembled. When the animal takes the bait, it pushes the trigger stick, which releases the weight to fall on its head.

A snare trap does not use bait. It is used on animal paths to snare the creatures as they go about their routine business. A snare trap is simple to build, but it does require string or cord to catch the animal.

Have you ever looped a rope on the floor or ground and, when someone stepped into it, yanked the rope to capture them? That is the principle behind the snare trap. To build one, you need a piece of string, a few small sticks to make a trigger, and a young tree that can be bent to provide spring for the trap.

Once you have found an animal run, pound two sticks into the ground next to the run or over the run. The sticks should be like upside down L-shapes. Next, find a small round stick that will fit under the lips of the two sticks. This is your trigger. To hold the trigger in place, tie string to a sapling and bend it over the trap, then tie the small round stick to the string and slip it between the stakes, which have been driven in the ground to hold the tension in the sapling. Next, tie a loop knot to the trigger stick and spread it open over the run. You will need to use twigs to hold the loop open. You can adjust the loop and trap to fit the type of animal you are trapping.

This type of snare trap is called a pencil snare trap.

Here are two suggestions for the described traps. If you build a deadfall, block one side with sticks so that the animal does not take the bait and run away before the weight drops. With the snare trap, you can drive stakes into the ground to funnel animals into the trap.

While it is okay to practice building these kinds of traps, and your family may even own a few traps for hunting, you must remember that these two traps are illegal except in survival situations. In any other situation you should obey your state's hunting laws.

There are many good books on surviving in the wilderness. Some of the best are written by Tom Brown. You might want to read *Tom Brown's Field Guide to Wilderness Survival* by Tom Brown, Jr. (with Brandt Morgan), or *Tom Brown's Field Guide to Nature and Survival for Children* (with Judy Brown). Brown has written several nature books and they are all excellent.

If you have decided that you can do without hunting animals for survival, here are two excellent books for you to read; *Euell Gibbons's Handbook of Edible Wild Plants,* by Euell Gibbons and Gordon Tucker, and *Edible Wild Plants,* by Oliver Perry Medsger.

The best way to learn about mountain survival is by trying some of the techniques discussed in this book. Try camping in your backyard for a weekend. Build a solar still and a camp fire, and cook something over the fire for practice. (Get your parents' permission before trying any of these things.)

Chapter 10
A Few Friendly Knots

Most people think anyone can tie a knot. It's simple! Maybe that's why nobody takes the time to learn how to use specific knots for specific purposes. But to be safe in the mountains, you should take the time to learn how to tie a few knots that will serve specific purposes. You will need to know three kinds of knots.

1) Knots to tie two pieces of rope together.
2) Knots to attach rope to other objects.
3) Knots for lashing things together.

It is fun to learn how to tie knots. Try it. Once you have mastered a few you will be able to pass on your knowledge to others.

Clove Hitch
This is a good knot for tying anything to a pole or post.

Make two loops.   *Place loop 1 over loop 2.*   *Slip over the pole or post.*   *Pull both ends of rope tight.*

Heaving Line Bend

For tying two ropes of different thickness together.

Carrick Bend

This is the best way of tying two ropes together.

Make a loop.

Second rope across the loop.

Weave together as shown.

Cross back over itself and out under the loop.

Sheepshank

You can use this method to shorten a rope or to strengthen a worn-out section in the middle of a rope.

Make a Z.

Loop the lower free ends as shown.

Repeat to fix a loop over the lower loop.

Square lashing

This looks more complicated than it really is. Square lashing is the best way to join two sticks together at right angles.

Tie a clove hitch.

Twist the short end of the cord so it doesn't hang loose.

Take the cord behind the cross pole.

 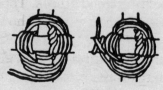

Now, take it down over the left side of the cross pole and behind the upright. Pull tight.

Repeat this three times more.

Take the cord back around the upright.

Wind round twice more.

Finish with a clove hitch.

Chapter 11
Map and Compass

For mountain hikers, campers, climbers, and adventurers, there is no better kind of map than the topographical type. In the United States, just about every inch of the country has been surveyed by government workers, and the details of the shape, slope, and height of mountains recorded. These are called United States Geological Survey maps. In Britain these maps are called ordinance survey maps.

These maps not only tell you about the mountains, but also show you the features of the land—where it is flat or hilly, where there are forests, rivers, parks, or towns. Each map covers a small area in great detail, so you may need two or three maps, depending on the amount of territory you plan to cover. They can be purchased at most book and sporting good stores. Topographical maps are useful for hikers because they show the contours of the terrain.

If you have a map, any kind of map, get it out and take a look at it. All maps have a few things in common that you should know about. First, there will be a boxed-in area with many bits of useful information. This is the key. Different map keys may have different symbols, depending on the type of map. For example, if you are looking at a highway map, the symbols will show you what types of lines are used to represent major highways, two-lane roads, secondary roads, railroad tracks, rivers, etc.

The key on a topographical map will usually have symbols for roads, paths, woods, rivers, marsh, or any special features, such as ruins. You must learn the symbols to understand the map.

Another useful item on all maps is a scale. Maps are drawn to scale so that you can use them to figure out the distance between places. In order to do this you use the scale. The scale shows you what distance is represented by a unit of measurement on the map. Scale is just a way of making the map fit the page. Some maps represent only a small area, like your neighborhood, while other maps may represent a whole state or country. Each map will have a scale to allow you to figure out distances between places, objects, or things represented on the map.

Two other features of maps are important. They tell you which directions things face. This is done by a north, south, east, west, marker. National Geographic maps often have these crossed arrows to show direction. If the map does not show the points of the compass, it is understood that the top of the map represents north.

Finally, most maps, except ancient treasure maps, will have a series of lines, evenly spaced, that run horizontally and vertically. This is called a grid. Each grid line across the top and side of the map is given a reference number, or letter of the alphabet. The purpose of a grid is to allow you to find points on the map more easily and give the position by using the reference letter and number.

Say you are looking for a certain street on your map. You know the name of the street but do not know where it is located in the town. City and town maps always have an index of street names. Your friends Christopher and Gabriel live on North Fayston Road. When you look in the index you find North Fayston Road is located at G 3 on the map. Across the top of the map you see that the vertical grid lines are lettered A, B, C, etc. You move your finger across the top until you reach G. Looking on the left side of the map, you see that the horizontal lines are numbered. Moving your finger down the G line till it intercepts the 3 line will show you the area where North Fayston Road is located.

Maybe you are planning a trip with a friend, a hike in the mountains. You have your topographical map in front of you and find the mountain you want to explore. You telephone your friend and tell her you have found the perfect mountain for your day's adventure.

"Where is it?" she asks.

You look at your map and find the location. "B 8," you tell her.

"Yes, I've found it," she says.

Spend some time looking at different kinds of maps. Learn how they represent the real world. The effort is fun and worthwhile when planning trips.

Compasses tell you which direction is north by means of a magnetized needle. The face of the compass is circular, with the four compass points N, S, E, W, marked off at ninety degree intervals. These four main points are known as the cardinal points. Once you know which direction north is, you can find any direction you want by using the compass. Besides being divided into 360 degrees (a circle) a compass gives a total of thirty-two direction points, including the four cardinal points.

If you are lost in the mountains, a compass cannot tell

you where you are, but it can show you which direction is which. If you know that a road is to the south, then you can use your compass to stay on course and walk south. The compass is also useful in making detours. It is not always possible to keep to one direction. If you encounter something that you must walk around, the compass allows you to make a change in direction and then get back on course.

A compass can help you find your location on a map if you know how to take a bearing. This requires a landmark that you can identify. If you are lost but can see the peak of old Mt. Reliable in the distance, then you can take a bearing and find your location on your map.

Here's how to do it. First hold your compass level and wait for the needle to settle down and point towards the magnetic north. (Keep it away from metal objects that might distort the magnetic field.) With the N mark lined up with the needle, look at old Mt. Reliable and imagine a straight line running from the center of the compass to the mountain. Look at the point where the line crosses the degree marks that circle the compass. This is the number of degrees old Mt. Reliable is from due north.

Now, get out your map, spread it flat, and line up the north-south grid mark with the north-pointing needle. Next, find Mt. Reliable on the map. Since you have calculated the degrees-from-north of Mt. Reliable, you can now place the compass on the map with the degree line aimed at Mt. Reliable. This is where you are. Look at the map and figure out how to get back to civilization.

There are other ways of finding directions without a compass. Here are a few that are good to know. (Because I live in the United States, I'm going to give examples for the northern hemisphere.)

The easiest is simply to use the sun. If you have a watch, the sun is always due south when it is twelve noon. Simple. Another way of using the great solar direction finder is to push a stick into the ground—make sure it is upright—and mark the tip of its shadow. Now wait a while, at least fifteen minutes. Now mark the tip of the new shadow. Draw a line on the ground connecting the two points. You have created an east-west line. The first shadow you marked was west and the second east. Draw a perpendicular line for north and south.

You can use your watch and the sun to find your direction any time of the day. Just line up the hour hand (the small hand) with the sun. Halfway between the hour hand and twelve is south. Say it's four in the afternoon. You line up the hour hand with the sun and look at your watch. The two o'clock position is south, and because you know this, you can figure the eight o'clock position is north.

At night, you can use the Big Dipper to find north. Just find the Big Dipper, then look at the two stars that form the end of the bowl farthest from the handle. Imagine a line running from the bottom star through the top star in the Dipper bowl, follow it out and you will see that it leads you to the North Star. Another way is to imagine the two stars lining up to point at the North Star.

The North Star is one of the brightest stars in the sky. It shines above the North Pole, and on clear nights is easy to spot. If you have trouble finding it, ask your parents, or a friend, to help you locate the North Star. Once you find it you can always find your way.

Chapter 12

Lost in the Mountains

Have you ever seen movies where people are lost, and when they try to find their way to civilization, they end up back at the same spot? Walking in circles is a problem for anyone lost in the mountains. Seriously. The reason, I've been told, is that people favor their right or left side. If you are right-handed, you will tend to walk in clockwise circles, if left-handed, counterclockwise circles. I'll tell you later how to avoid this problem.

Thousands of people get lost in the mountains every year. They are usually once-a-year vacationers or weekend hikers who set off exploring. Now, there is nothing wrong with exploring. It's one of the main attractions of going to the mountains. Getting lost is another matter.

One way to avoid getting lost is to take a few simple precautions when you are looking over new territory. If you are trailblazing—making your own new trail—take the time to leave trail markers so that you can retrace your steps. Make mental note of landmarks as you hike: a mountain peak in the distance, or a large rock, a tree that has an unusual shape, even the smell of flowers in a mountain meadow. From time to time, stop and look back to see where you've been. It's good to know what the way back looks like.

Mt. Hilliers, a domed mountain, in the Henry Mountain Resource Area in Utah.

(Bureau of Land Management)

When I was in grade school, our class went on a field trip to a science museum. One of the exhibits had to do with the sense of sight and sound. A kind of fun house maze had been constructed to demonstrate the importance of sight. One by one, we were invited to make our way through the maze. Inside it was totally dark. My first reaction was normal—I panicked. Unable to see anything, I took a stumbling step forward, my heart beating like crazy. Using my hands to guide me, I managed to make several wrong turns and walked into several walls. Eventually, I made it out the other end and turned down the offer to make the trip a second time. Enough was enough.

That experience taught me a lot about finding my way in the mountains—that first, most people don't take the time to observe their surroundings. I don't think people have a built-in sense of direction. We must rely on observation of details that will help us find our way. Second, that my first reaction of panic had to be overcome in order to profit from the learning experience of the maze.

You can mark a trail the way the trailblazing pioneers did for the people who would follow. They built cairns, simple piles of rocks left at intervals to mark the way. Less permanent trail markers take no time at all: simply scuff marks into the earth from time to time or use sticks to make arrow markers on the ground. You can mark a tree with your pocket knife every so often, but remember, you don't want to hurt the tree, so do not cut through the bark.

Now, what happens if you get lost? You will probably feel a rush of panic. This is natural, but after you have taken note of your feelings, tell yourself to calm down. Your friends and family know you are in the mountains, so your job is to stay safe. People will be looking for you when you don't return. Remember, your task is survival.

In a survival situation, your first objective is protection from the elements. Build a shelter, assess water needs, and if necessary build a solar still, collect firewood, and inventory food supplies. Stay out of the wind and rain. If the weather is cold, don't sit on exposed ground or bare rocks without some sort of insulation. Conserve your energy. Think before you act, and that way you won't be wasting body heat.

If you don't have food, it doesn't mean survival is im-

A view of the Mormon Range, east of Las Vegas, Nevada. These are faulted mountains.

(Courtesy of the Department of Library Services, American Museum of Natural History, Neg. No. 332977, Photo: Chris Schuberth)

possible. With adequate shelter and water you can function for several days without food. The important thing is to keep warm. Your biggest concern should be preventing exposure or hypothermia. The symptoms of hypothermia are fatigue, shivering, lack of coordination, disorientation, drowsiness, and blue skin.

If you're lost, you should think about letting searchers know where you are. First, if you have a piece of bright material such as a handkerchief, you should attach it to a stick and hoist it over your camp. It is very difficult to spot a natural shelter because it blends into the surroundings. This marker also makes it easy for you to find your way back after searching for food or water.

The best way of letting people know where you are is with a signal fire. The difference between a regular camp fire and a signal fire is that the signal fire produces a lot of smoke. Once you have a camp fire going, you want to feed it with green and wet wood. This will produce a smoky fire that is easy for searchers to spot. Be careful that you don't put the fire out; you must maintain the fire with pieces of dry wood, adding the green or wet wood when necessary.

If you see an airplane passing over your location but think that it doesn't see you, you can produce great billows of smoke by adding wet leaves to your fire. Another way to let aircraft know where you are is to use large stones to spell out a message in a clearing.

Look for a clear level patch of ground and use whatever you can find to spell out your message. What should you spell? SOS. The three letters SOS are recognized as a distress signal throughout the world. They really stand for "save our ship," but have come to be recognized as a signal for help.

Did you know that on a clear day the flash from sunlight reflected off a mirror can be seen for more than twenty miles? A hand mirror makes an excellent signaling device. To use a hand mirror correctly, hold the mirror at eye level, facing the sun so that the light is reflected off the glass. Your free hand acts as a sight.

Let's say you see an airplane in the distance and want to signal it. Hold your free hand, at arm's length, between you and the airplane. You can leave your fingers spread to keep the airplane in sight. Next, tilt the mirror until the reflected light hits your outstretched hand. Now take your hand away and the light is directed right at the airplane. You can practice sighting with a mirror anytime the sun is out. Keep in mind while you are practicing you are doing just that—practicing. Do not flash light into the eyes of car drivers or at airplanes overhead. They may be startled or even think you *are* in trouble.

You can signal messages with a mirror, or a whistle, using the Morse code. Morse code is an international signaling language based on short signals (dots) and long signals (dashes). Different combinations of dots and dashes represent different letters of the alphabet. You can use long and short flashes from a mirror, or long and short notes on a whistle, to send messages. (The Morse for SOS is dot dot dot dash dash dash dot dot dot.)

By nature humans are impatient. We don't like to wait for someone to find us while we sit in our camp doing nothing. The best advice is to stay put. But you can look for help in two ways: first, by climbing to a higher location to take a look around, and second, by taking short exploratory walks away from your camp in different directions. There are drawbacks to both choices.

First, when climbing a tree or climbing to higher ground to look around, you risk injury. (Also, remember that the higher up the mountain, the colder the air.) A twisted ankle can be life-threatening when you are on your own in a survival situation. So take care in finding a vantage point.

The second choice of short forays away from your survival camp to look for help could lead to your getting lost again. Remember the walking-in-circles problem. The way to avoid this is to decide on the direction you are going to take, then sight a tree or some other object a hundred or so feet away. When you reach that tree, look

The Morse Code

A	. _
B	_ . . .
C	_ . _ .
D	_ . .
E	.
F	. . _ .
G	_ _ .
H	. . . .
I	. .
J	. _ _ _
K	_ . _
L	. _ . .
M	_ _
N	_ .
O	_ _ _
P	. _ _ .
Q	_ _ . _
R	. _ .
S	. . .
T	_
U	. . _
V	. . . _
W	. _ _
X	_ . . _
Y	_ . _ _
Z	_ _ . .

back and use your camp and the tree to line up another tree a hundred feet or so away. You mark each tree so that you can find your way back. This method of sighting from tree to tree guarantees that you walk in a straight line.

When lost in the mountains, you may be closer to civilization than you think. At night, lights can be seen from a great distance. If you see a light, mark the direction of the light on the ground, then try and determine what the light represents—house, city, car, etc.—and how far away it is. If you are careful in noting the location of the light, you can try signaling the next day with your mirror. Or you might want to try walking out.

Finally, if possible, you should walk down the mountain as far as possible before setting up a base camp to wait for help. There are two reasons why you should walk *down* the mountain rather than *up*. First, the higher up the mountain you are, the colder the temperature. Many people when lost in the mountains will want to walk to higher ground for the vantage point. This is a mistake. It is okay to walk higher to look around, but this should be done after you have established a camp. Second, water is usually in the valleys. By walking down the mountain you increase your chances of finding water.

If you find water, a stream or river, and can't sit still and wait for help, walk along the riverbank. Water usually leads to civilization.

You have already read the chapters on finding your way in the mountains. The information about using maps and compasses, as well as the sun and stars, for finding direction is very useful and should prevent your getting lost. Or, if you do become lost, help you find your way out. And remember: don't panic, and keep warm.

Chapter 13

Survival Kits

Being prepared for survival situations takes some planning. Making sure that you have the right tools to survive can save your life in a risky situation. It's fun to pack a survival kit. You can modify yours to suit your specific needs. The following are some suggestions for several survival kits.

The Basic Survival Kit

These items are considered essential in all kits:

- **Matches**—you can buy waterproof matches at a sporting goods store or you can make waterproof matches by dripping melted candle wax over the match heads. You just scratch off the wax when you need a light. Even better, I think, is to simply store the "strike anywhere" kind of kitchen matches in a plastic film container. The kind that thirty-five millimeter film comes in is perfect.

- **Compass**—if possible, get the kind that has a plastic flip-up cover, which protects the glass and makes the compass more rugged. Don't buy a toy compass. A good compass only costs a few dollars and is worth it.

- **Candle**—a candle is cheap, easy to carry, and a good source of light and even heat. It doesn't require batteries.

- **A small mirror**—you can use it to check to make sure your teeth are clean, or comb your hair, or use it for signaling.

- **Pocket knife**—The Swiss army kind have all kinds of gadgets, but they cost a lot of money. If you can afford one, fine—but if not, a simpler version will work just fine.

- **Water-collecting materials**—A lightweight sheet of plastic for making a solar still. Remember, the water you collect in your solar still is clean and drinkable, but you might also want to take along some water purification tablets (buy them in a drug store or sporting supply store) for water you collect from other sources. Another good idea, but not essential, is to carry a sponge in your survival kit. A sponge can be used to collect dew efficiently.

- **Twine or strong cord**—There are many strong, lightweight, nylon cords on the market that hold incredible amounts of weight. You should check at a sporting goods store that specializes in mountaineering. Strong nylon cord can be used in a variety of survival situations. For example, you can use it for fishing line, to build fish traps, for lashing things together, to make a bow, for snare traps, and for climbing. Remember, it should be strong and lightweight.

This looks like a lot, but everything listed above will fit into a ziplock bag. With these few items, you can ensure that you have fire, water, and shelter. You can signal help in an emergency situation. It's worth the time, and a lot of fun, too, to put together your own survival kit.

You can adapt the basic kit to meet your specific needs. Here are some other items that you might want to add to the survival items listed above to make a *super* survival kit. (I have a pocket survival kit that I carry in a tin tobacco box. It's just the right size and doesn't take up too much room. You might want to look around for a pocket-sized tin box to hold your kit.)

The Deluxe Kit

- **A penlight**—those tiny little flashlights that are about the size of a pen. Make sure you use alkaline batteries; they last longer.

- **Flexible wire saw**—this is a piece of sharp wire, about a foot or so in length, with a handhold ring at each end. It can be rolled up and stored in your pocket survival kit. You can use it to saw small branches.

- **Fish hooks and a fishing line**—a few hooks shoved into a cork will do. The cork will keep the hooks from rattling around or biting you, and it also serves other purposes. You can wind some fishing line around the cork. You don't need hundreds of feet. If you want to fish, just use a branch to hold the line in the water; the cork can be used as a bobber.

- **Disinfectant wipes and a few Band-Aids**—You can get disinfectant wipes in drugstores and most supermarkets. They are usually packaged in individual foil packets, making them easy to carry and preventing them from drying out.
- **Needle and thread**—always good to have.
- **Magnifying glass**—you can use it to study nature or start a fire. The cheap kind are fine.

The Super Deluxe Survival Pack

Here are some items you might want to include for the ultimate in survival kits. Your choice of items will depend on how long you are going to be in the mountains and weather conditions. Think about these items and decide if they should be in your survival kit.

- **Insect repellent**—There are many types on the market. I don't like the feel of insect repellent on my skin, but sometimes it is necessary. For example, if you are hiking in New England in May, the mayflies can be more bothersome than the insect repellent. Remember, all repellents should be kept away from your eyes and out of your mouth. A possibly useful gadget is a tiny electronic repellent device that looks like a pen and has a pocket clip, making it easy to carry. It is supposed to repel mosquitoes—probably the most universal of pesky insects—but I'm not sure how effective it is. Check with your sporting goods store for availability.
- **Sunscreen**—Because the air is thinner at higher altitudes, more ultraviolet rays are bombarding you

when you are high in the mountains. Even when it is cold the rays are getting through.

- **Solar Blanket**—This is a very lightweight, thin, plastic-like blanket (sometimes made out of Mylar, a plastic fabric you may have seen in shiny helium-filled balloons) that reflects the body's heat back in towards itself. They are cheap and disposable.
- **First aid kit**—the items to be included are at the end of the next chapter on first aid.

A few words about survival foods:

Always take some food when you go on an expedition in the mountains. It doesn't have to take up a lot of room, and can come in handy in an emergency. If nothing else, a few pieces of hard candy could provide the extra bit of energy you might need to make it down the mountain.

You should always choose foods that provide the most energy in the most compact form for your survival supply:

- Nuts
- Dried fruits
- Powdered milk
- Dried soups
- Dried meats (beef jerky)

The above foods are available in most supermarkets. Camping stores have a variety of interesting, well-balanced, dehydrated meals that you might want to check out. Just choose a few items to make sure your survival kit is not too heavy.

Chapter 14

Mountain Medic
(Basic First Aid Skills)

Some of the stuff I talk about in this chapter is pretty gory but it is information you should understand before going into the mountains. If you, or someone with you, is injured, you want to be able to treat the problem on the spot. This is first aid. You may require medical attention for some injuries, but first aid may keep the injury from getting worse. As you can see by its name, it is the aid that is given first.

Here are some words of caution before I get started on specific types of injuries. *Avoiding* problems is the ultimate first aid, and there are things you can do to cut down on injuries. Check the weather report and dress properly for the season and the altitude. This is common sense, but remember what happened on Mt. San Gorgonio.

Wear good comfortable hiking shoes. They don't have to be heavy boots; there are many good lightweight hiking and climbing shoes available through shoe stores and mountain shops. Wear the shoes around a few days before heading into the mountains. Blisters are a major problem for hikers and climbers, so be sure your shoes fit properly and are comfortable. Don't wear moccasin-type shoes. A good pair of jogging or hiking sneakers is better than any pair of moccasins you can find.

Watch where you're going. Again, this is common sense advice, but a broken or twisted ankle can mean you spend the night in the mountains, unable to move, waiting for the rescue team. Don't forget—be sure people know when you are leaving and the approximate time of your return. Also, let them know the mountain area you will be exploring, and be as specific as possible. And remember, don't go hiking or climbing alone. Always hike or climb with a companion.

The following is information about treating common injuries. If you don't know what the injury is, don't try to treat it. You could do more harm than good.

• Cuts, Wounds, and Bleeding

Our outer layer of skin is a protective covering. When it is broken, blood escapes. Blood circulates in our body by way of arteries, veins, and capillaries. Bleeding is caused when one of these blood vessels is broken. If an artery or vein is punctured a lot of blood may be lost. Major blood loss can cause a person to go into shock or even die, so it is important to stop the bleeding as soon as possible.

The best way to stop the blood flow is by direct pressure on the wound. If possible, raise the injured part above the heart to reduce blood flow to the area, and then apply pressure. You may have to apply pressure for several minutes to stop the flow of blood. Another way of applying pressure is to bandage the wound with a sterile dressing or piece of cloth. If the blood soaks through the bandage, don't try and remove it. That could start the blood flowing again. You can wrap the wound with another bandage.

If something is sticking in the wound, don't try to remove it. Pulling it out may cause the blood to flow more freely by doing more damage. If a lot of blood is lost, treat for shock.

• Hypothermia

If you lose body heat rapidly it can kill you. Hypothermia is caused most often by a combination of factors including cold, wetness, wind, and exhaustion. The symptoms begin with feeling cold and progress to shivering, slower reflexes, loss of balance, blurred vision, and possible collapse or loss of consciousness. The combination of high altitude and cold winds can be deadly.

The loss of core body heat must be treated quickly. Get the person into a warm environment, and wrap him or her with blankets or get the person into an insulated sleeping bag. If you have them, give the person hot liquids such as sugared tea or broth, even hot or warm water. If the person is walking, stop him or her. Walking uses up vital energy.

• Burns

When you're in the thin mountain air, you are being bombarded by more ultraviolet rays than at ground level. The chances of getting sunburned are increased because the higher up the mountain, the cooler the temperature and the thinner the air. In other words, you won't feel hot, like you're burning. So be careful. Other sources of burns are camp fires and hot objects such as cooking utensils.

You should use sunscreen when hiking or climbing

in the summer. If you get sunburned, there are commercial treatments that are soothing. But remember to keep the burned area covered and out of the sun until your skin has healed.

If you are burned by a fire or hot object, cool the burned area by holding it in running water for ten to fifteen minutes. If you don't have running water, soak the burned area. Never put butter or fats on a burn. Don't put anything sticky on the burned area. If you have gauze, dress the burned area; you can also use a clean handkerchief or piece of cloth. If the burned area develops blisters, don't pop them. This could cause infections. If you are burned badly you should see a doctor.

- **Blisters**

This seems like a minor problem, but if you are hiking blistered feet can cause you to be miserable. (Remember to wear your hiking or climbing shoes or sneakers a few days, minimum, before setting out for the mountains.) If you get a blister on your foot, don't pop it. Cover it with a bandage and make sure your socks are clean. Try to figure out what's causing your feet to blister. Sometimes an extra pair of socks helps if your foot is slipping inside your shoe. If the blister pops by itself, keep it clean and covered.

- **Broken bones**

When a bone breaks it is called a fracture. You can sometimes hear the bone break. A fractured limb, such as an ankle, may be twisted or bent at an odd angle. The area around the break will probably swell up, and the area will become discolored.

If you think you or someone you're with has broken

a bone, don't try to move. *Never* move. Some books recommend splinting a fracture—that is, using something to support the broken area—but I think it best to get as comfortable as possible and wait for a doctor. If you are alone and injured, try to stretch out. Cover yourself with whatever you can find that will keep you warm. (It is always good to carry a solar blanket on outings.) If you are with someone who is injured, get a doctor or rescue team.

- **Heat stroke**

    Sometimes when you're hiking or climbing you can become overheated. This causes the body's natural cooling mechanisms to work inefficiently. This happens most often in hot, humid climates, so the risk is not great for mountain climbers unless you are in a tropical mountain range such as those found in South America.

    When someone is overheated he or she becomes dizzy, the pulse quickens, the skin becomes flushed, and the person feels hot, or overheated. The victim can faint or become unconscious from overheating.

    The treatment is the opposite of that for hypothermia. Get the person to a cool, shady spot. Sponge the person with cool water. Fan the person. Get medical assistance if necessary.

- **Shock**

    If someone loses a lot of blood or suffers from internal bleeding, he or she may go into shock. Another cause of shock is a massive injury, such as a broken ankle, or a fall that does internal damage. Technically, shock occurs when the body's organs are deprived of oxygen.

111

First Aid Kit

When putting together your survival equipment, be sure to include a first aid kit. It will be useful in treating minor problems that occur from time to time when you are in the mountains, such as insect bites, blisters, cuts, and scratches. Hopefully, you won't have major injuries. The following is a list of things you might want to include in your kit:

- Gauze for dressing burns and wounds.
- Roll of bandage tape.
- Aspirin.
- Sunblock cream.
- Antiseptic towelettes.
- Calamine lotion for insect bites.
- Antibacterial cream for use on open wounds and blisters.
- Insect repellent.
- Germicidal soap for washing hands before treating wounds.
- Scissors.
- Tweezers.
- Safety pins.
- Elastic bandage for minor sprains.
- First aid book.

You can use the above list as a guide to create a kit that meets your specific needs. Remember, prevention is the best treatment.

The symptoms of shock are cold, sweaty skin; the victim looks pale, has shallow, fast breathing, or may be yawning and sighing because of lack of air. The pulse will be weak and rapid, and the person may pass out.

If the person is bleeding, stop the bleeding. Lay the person down and try to get the feet slightly higher than the head. This is better for circulation. Keep the patient warm and as comfortable as possible. You should get a doctor or rescue team.

- **Altitude sickness**

This is caused by the thin air at high altitudes. The body requires some time to adapt to the changes in oxygen content when we climb very tall mountains. This will probably never be a problem you experience in recreational climbing or hiking. But if you get the opportunity to hike or climb a mountain that is a real monster, you should be aware of the symptoms. The most common symptoms are usually headache and fatigue. At really high altitudes (above 20,000 feet), people can become disoriented and even hallucinate.

In most cases, the treatment is simple. Turn around and descend until the symptoms disappear. You can stop and let your body get used to the new level, before returning back up the mountain. This could be anything from a short stop of an hour or so up to several days.

Climbers in the Himalayas often work their way up through a series of camps, spending from one to several days at each new height. They also carry bottled oxygen.

Chapter 15

The Mountains Near Home

My son Gabe had spent two weeks making the longbow out of a young ironwood sapling. He had peeled the bark and let the bow season before shaping, and finally stringing it against the natural bend of the wood. It was a fine bow.

We packed the night before and left before dawn the next morning. While I sipped my coffee, and drove through the streaky predawn darkness, he slept in the seat beside me. At twelve, he was big for his age and strong, and from his shoe size it looked like there was a lot of growing left.

I half expected the rangers to remember me, but of course they didn't. Everything had changed since I climbed the mountain with my brother years before. Everything except the mountain. After checking in, Gabe rolled out the maps, and with his finger, traced the line we would follow up the mountain.

The weather reporter on the radio said the weekend would be warm and sunny. After a diner breakfast of pancakes and eggs, we set off for the mountain. My backpack was loaded with layers of warm clothing—it would be cold at the top—freeze-dried food, a gas cooker and lamp, first aid kit, and survival pack. Besides his bow and arrows, Gabe carried the lightweight nylon tent and our sleeping bags in his pack.

The early part of the climb was good. We stopped several times to collect plants or look at rocks or to rest. At midday we stopped and ate the sandwiches we had packed that morning. The sun was warm, and in the distance we could hear the rippling hiss of a mountain stream.

We camped at a clearing just below the timberline. There were so many stars it looked as if a bag of shiny pebbles had been broken above us. After dinner, we talked about the upcoming day's climb, how we would climb to the top and take pictures of each other.

Before turning in for the night, I showed Gabe how to store our food by hanging it from a tree branch, to keep animals from stealing it while we slept. After that we tucked ourselves into our sleeping bags and tried to settle down.

"I'm really tired," Gabe said, "but it feels good."

"Me, too," I said.

After a while, he asked, "Why is camping so much fun?"

"It's like anything else," I said, "the more you know about it, the more you enjoy it."

"So, knowing something about the different kinds of trees, and animals, and rocks, makes camping enjoyable?"

"Yes. And knowing about the history of the place, the environment, and the habits of the creatures that live here, all add to the enjoyment."

"Why?"

"Because when we know these things they become part of us. Then we feel more than safe in the mountains. We feel at home."

"Makes sense to me," he said.

It took a while for Gabe to get to sleep. I looked out into the clear night. While we had talked, the moving earth had changed the pattern of the stars overhead.

In the morning, we hiked to the top of the mountain. After taking pictures, we hiked back to our camp and packed up our gear. The trip had been fun because we had come prepared.

We headed down the mountain. Everything had been perfect.

Some Good Books

Fiction

The Sign of the Beaver by Elizabeth George Speare

Nonfiction

About the mountains, *The Mountains,* part of the Time-Life series.

About camping, *An Usborne Guide, Camping and Walking,* by David Watkins and Meike Dalal.

About survival, *Tom Brown's Field Guide To Wilderness Survival,* by Tom Brown, Jr. with Brandt Morgan.

Also about survival, *Improve Your Survival Skills,* by Lucy Smith, an Usborne Superskills book.

About foraging for food, *Stalking The Wild Asparagus,* by Euell Gibbons.

About nature, *The Amateur Naturalist,* by Gerald Durrell.

There are many excellent field guides available that teach you to identify trees, shrubs, wild flowers, birds, plants, and animals. These are often regional guides, designed to teach you about your area of the country.

The Peterson field guides and the Audubon field guides are both wonderful sources of information. Look in your library and bookstore for a guide that suits your particular needs.

Date Due

BRODART, CO.   Cat. No. 23-233-003   Printed in U.S.A.